Preface

Aim

The aim of the *Essential Elements* series is to provide course support material covering the main subject areas of HND/C Business Studies and equivalent level courses at a price that students can afford. Students can select titles to suit the requirements of their own particular courses whether BTEC Certificate in Business Administration, Certificate in Marketing, IPS Foundation, Institute of Bankers, Access to Business Studies, Institute of Personnel Management, or other appropriate undergraduate and professional courses.

Many courses now have a modular structure, i.e. individual subjects are taught in a relatively short period of, say, 10 to 12 weeks. The *Essential Elements* series meets the need for material which can be built into the students' study programmes and used for directed self-study. All the texts, therefore, include activities with answers for students' self-assessment, activities for lecturer-assessment, and references to further reading.

The series is a joint venture between DP Publications and South Birmingham College.

How to use the series

All the books in the series are intended to be used as workbooks and provide approximately 70 hours of study material. Each text covers the essential elements of that subject, so that the core of any course at this level is covered, leaving the lecturer to add supplementary material if required. All have the following features:

❏ **In-text activities,** which aim to promote understanding of the principles, and are set at frequent intervals in the text. The solutions add to the student's knowledge, as well as providing an introduction to the next learning point.

❏ **End of chapter exercises**, some of which are intended for self-assessment by the student (these have solutions at the back of the book). Others are suitable for setting by the lecturer and answers or marking guides are provided in the Lecturers' Supplement. These exercises include progress and review questions, multiple choice questions, which test specific knowledge and allow rapid marking, practice questions, questions for advanced students, and assignments.

❏ **Further reading references** for students who wish to follow up particular topics in more depth.

❏ **Lecturers' Supplement**, which is available free of charge to lecturers adopting the book as a course text. It includes answers or guides to marking to help with student assessment.

Other titles in the series

Available 1994: Business Economics, Business Planning and Policy, Financial Accounting, Management Accounting, Quantitative Methods.

Available 1995: Business Law, Human Resource Management, Management Information Systems, Marketing.

Contents

1   *Survey methods*

1.1 *Introduction*

Many decisions made by business and the government are the result of information obtained from surveys. Newspapers commission opinion polls in order to forecast the result of an election or a company may want to measure consumer's reaction to a new product. Surveys are carried out on a sample of people and the purpose of this chapter is to look at the different methods of obtaining this sample. Methods of analysing a sample will be discussed in subsequent chapters.

At the end of this chapter you should be able to:

❐ Understand the difference between a population and a sample

❐ Understand the difference between probabilistic and non-probabilistic sampling methods

❐ Choose the correct sampling method for different situations

1.2 *The basics of sampling*

I am sure that you have been a *respondent* in a survey at least once in your life. Have you filled in a *questionnaire* or been stopped in the street and asked some questions? You no doubt know that the purpose of a survey is for some organisation or person to obtain *information* about some issue or product. This information could range from what television programme you watched last night to your views on the government of the day. A survey only collects information about a small subset of the population. The population can and often does refer to all the people in Britain or a town but for statisticians it is also a very general term to refer to all groups or items being surveyed. For instance it could refer to the viewing habits of all children in a town or as you will see in a later chapter, it could refer to the weights of jars of coffee produced by a company during a week. The alternative to a survey is to question every member of the population and when this done it is called a *census*. Unfortunately it is expensive and very difficult to carry out a census and also unnecessary. A survey of a small subset of the population, called a *sample* can give surprisingly accurate results if carried out properly. Unfortunately if not carried out correctly the results can at best be unreliable and at the worst misleading. Before you carry out a survey you need answers to several questions, such as:

    ❐ What is the purpose of this survey?

    ❐ What is my target population?

    ❐ Do I have a list of the population?

    ❐ How can I avoid bias in my sample?

    ❐ How accurate do I want my survey to be?

    ❐ What resources do I have at my disposal?

    ❐ How am I going to collect the required data?

It is crucial to be clear about the purpose of the survey. Not only will this dictate your target population but it will also allow you to formulate your questionnaire correctly.

For example, if you are interested in consumer's opinion of a new alcoholic drink it would be pointless targeting people under 18 (and unethical). The target population should contain every person that it is likely to buy your product or whose views you are particularly interested in.

Once you have selected your target population you need to determine whether there is any list that would allow you to identify every member of the population. This list is called a *sampling frame* and without this the accuracy of your results can be seriously flawed. However, sometimes a sampling frame is simply not available or difficult to obtain, in which case achieving a representative sample will be more difficult, but not necessarily impossible.

Activity 1

What would be your target population for a survey on motorway tariffs and would there be a sampling frame available?

If you were only interested in the views of car drivers then anyone holding a UK driving licence would form your target population. A suitable sampling frame would be records held by the DVLC at Swansea. It will not be 100% accurate as drivers may have moved address and not informed the DVLC or died.

Once your target population has been chosen and an appropriate sampling frame identified, it is necessary to choose your sample. If the sample is chosen badly your results will be inaccurate due to *bias* in your sample. Bias is caused by choosing a sample that is unrepresentative of the target population. For example, perhaps you wanted to discover people's views on whether a sports field should be sold to a property developer. If your sample contained a large number of people from the local football club then the sample is likely to be biased in favour of one particular group! To avoid bias you need to ensure that your sample is *representative* of the target population. You will see how this can be achieved later.

The purpose of a survey is to obtain information about a population. All other things being equal, the accuracy of the sample results will depend on the sample size; the larger the sample the more accurate the results. A large sample will clearly cost more than a small one although the method that is employed to collect the data will also determine the accuracy and cost of the survey. Methods of data collection range from the use of postal questionnaires to 'face-to-face' interviews. Some methods of data collection are expensive but guarantee a good response rate while others are cheap to administer but are likely to produce quite a poor response. The table below compares the main methods of collecting data:

	Postal questionnaire	Telephone interviewing	Face-to-face interviewing
Cost	Low	Moderate	High
Response rate	Low	Moderate	High
Speed	Slow	Fast	Fast *
Quantity of information collected	Limited	Moderate	High
Quality of information collected	Depends on how well the questionnaire has been designed	Good	High

* The speed of collecting the data will be high but travelling time by the interviewers may need to be considered.

Activity 2

You have been asked to obtain views of the student population at your institution regarding car parking facilities within the campus. What method of data collection would you use?

The best method would probably be face-to-face interviews but it is unlikely that you would have the resources for this approach. Telephone interviewing is probably not realistic because not many students will be on the telephone. This leaves you with a postal questionnaire, which should be quite reasonable for this relatively simple type of survey.

There are two types of sampling procedures for obtaining your sample. The first is *probabilistic* sampling, which requires the existence of a sampling frame. The second method is *non-probabilistic* sampling, which does not rely on a sampling frame. Probabilistic sampling allows you to calculate the probability that any member of the population will be selected and this fact can be used to ensure that the sample is representative of the target population.

1.3 Simple random sampling

With this method every member of the target population has an *equal* chance of being selected. This implies that a sampling frame is required and a method of *randomly* selecting the required sample from this list. The simplest example of this technique is a raffle where the winning ticket is drawn from the 'hat'. For a more formal application a stream of *random numbers* would be used. Random numbers are numbers that show no pattern and each digit is equally likely. A table of random numbers is given in Appendix 2, page 138. The method of simple random sampling using random numbers is quite easy to apply, although tedious as you will see from the following example.

Example

The table below is a part of the list of the students enrolled on a business studies course at a university.

Number	Name	Sex
1	N. Adams	Male
2	C. Atley	Male
3	B. Booth	Female
4	C. Best	Male
5	A. Bently	Male
6	D. Drew	Male
7	K. Fisher	Female
8	P. Frome	Male
9	G. Godfrey	Male
10	J. Holmes	Male
11	D. Jeffrey	Female
12	H. Jones	Male
13	M. Jones	Male
14	N. King	Female
15	K. Lenow	Male
16	A. Loft	Female
17	T. Mate	Female
18	S. Moore	Female
19	F. Muper	Female
20	R. Muster	Female
21	A. Night	Male
22	J. Nott	Male
23	L. Nupper	Male
24	K. Oates	Male
25	O. Patter	Female

Say from this 'population' of 25 students you wanted to randomly select a sample of 5 students. How would you do it? You could use the student number (in this case conveniently numbered from 1 to 25) and then try and obtain a match using a stream of two digit random numbers. For example, suppose you had the following random numbers: 78, 41, 11, 62, 72, 18, 66, 69, 58, 71, 31, 90, 51, 36, 78, 09, 41, 00, 70, 50, 58, 19, 68, 26, 75, 69, and 04. The first two numbers don't exist in our population but 11 does- it is student D. Jeffrey. The next two numbers do not exist but 18 does and so on. The final sample is numbers 11, 18, 09, 19 and 04, which are students D. Jeffrey, S. Moore, G. Godfrey, F. Muper, and C. Best.

The majority of random numbers were redundant in this case because the population was so small. However, in practise the population would be much larger but the method remains essentially the same. Most sampling frames are held on computer these days so it is much easier to use the computer to select the sample.

Activity 3

Randomly select another sample of 5 students from the above list using the random numbers: 09, 55, 42, 30, 27, 05, 25, 93, 78, 10, 69, 09, and 11.

You should have noticed that number 09 occurs twice. What did you do in this case. For practical reasons you should have ignored the second 09 and chosen the next number 11 instead. Your final sample should have been: G. Godfrey, A. Bently, O. Patter, J. Holmes, and D. Jeffrey.

How representative of the target population are these samples? Since the population is so small it is a simple matter to compare each sample with the population. For instance there are 15 male and 10 female students, which is a proportion of 60% males to 40% females. In the first sample there was 2 males out of 5, a proportion of 40% and in the second there was 4 males, a proportion of 80%. From this you can see that the first sample was an underestimate of the true number of males, while the second was an overestimate. Another sample could be different again and you may even get a sample of all the same sex. This variation is called sampling error and occurs in all sampling procedures. In Chapter 6 you will be shown how to quantify this error.

It is possible to reduce the *sampling error* by a slight modification to the simple random sample method. This is applicable when the target population can be categorised into groups or *strata*.

1.4 Stratified sampling

Many populations can be divided into different categories. For example, a population of adults consists of the two sexes, the employed and unemployed and many other categories. If you think that the responses you will get from your survey are likely to be determined partly by each category then clearly you want your sample to contain each category in the correct proportions.

Activity 4

Using the random numbers 09, 55, 42, 30, 27, 05, 25, 93, 78, 10, 69, 09, 11, 99, 21, and 01 obtain a sample of size 5 that contains the correct proportion of each sex.

You probably realised that your sample should contain 3 males (60% of 5). In order to ensure that you will get exactly 3 males, you should first of all have separated out the two sexes and then obtained two simple random samples, one of size 3 and one of size 2 as follows:

Number	Name	Sex
1	N. Adams	Male
2	C. Atley	Male
3	C. Best	Male
4	A. Bently	Male
5	D. Drew	Male
6	P. Frome	Male
7	G. Godfrey	Male
8	J. Holmes	Male
9	H. Jones	Male
10	M. Jones	Male
11	K. Lenow	Male
12	A. Night	Male
13	J. Nott	Male
14	L. Nupper	Male
15	K. Oates	Male

1	O. Patter	Female
2	B. Booth	Female
3	K. Fisher	Female
4	D. Jeffrey	Female
5	N. King	Female
6	A. Loft	Female
7	T. Mate	Female
8	S. Moore	Female
9	F. Muper	Female
10	R. Muster	Female

The two populations have been re-numbered although this is not essential. The first sample consists of students 9,5 and 10, that is H. Jones, D. Drew and M. Jones, while the second sample consists of 9 and 1, that is F. Muper and O. Patter.

Stratified sampling is a very reliable method but it does assume that you have a knowledge of the categories of the population. Stratified sampling is often used in conjunction with the next method.

1.5 Multi-stage sampling

If the target population covers a wide geographical area then a simple random sample may have selected respondents in quite different parts of the country. If the method employed to collect the data is of the face-to-face interview type then clearly a great deal of travelling could be involved. To overcome this problem the area to be surveyed is split up into smaller areas and a number of these smaller areas randomly selected. If desired the smaller areas chosen could themselves be divided into smaller districts and a random number of these selected. This procedure is continued until the area is small enough for a simple random sample (or a stratified sample) to be selected. The final sample should consist of respondents concentrated into a small number of areas. It is important that the random sample chosen from each area is the same proportion of the population or else bias towards certain areas could result. As it is bias is likely to occur as a result of similarity of responses from people within the same area, but this is the price you pay for reduced travelling time.

Activity 5

You have been asked to obtain a sample of television viewers from across Great Britain using the multi-stage sampling method. How would you select the sample?

The country could be split into counties or perhaps television regions may be more appropriate in this case. A number of these are chosen at random and these areas divided into district councils. A random sample of districts within each chosen region could now be selected and the selected districts divided into postal areas. The diagram below illustrates the case where HTV West is one of the chosen regions. Within this region, Northavon and Kingswood have been randomly selected and within Northavon the postal district of BS12 is one of the selected areas. A simple random sample of all household within BS12 could now be chosen and combined with all the other households chosen in other areas.

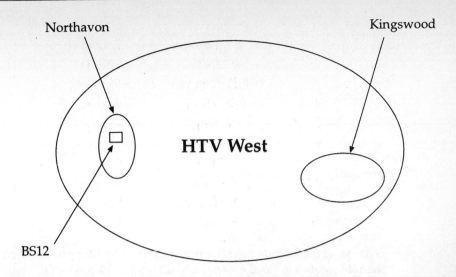

Northavon   Kingswood

HTV West

BS12

Figure 1

1.6 *Cluster sampling*

Cluster sampling is similar to multi-stage sampling and is used when a sampling frame is not available. Again a large geographical area is divided into a number of small areas called clusters. If necessary these clusters can be further subdivided to obtain clusters which are small enough for *all* members of the cluster to be surveyed. As with multi-stage sampling a bias will result due to similarities in responses from members of the same cluster. The difference between cluster sampling and multi-stage sampling is that since individual members of a cluster cannot be identified in advance, it is necessary for all members to be surveyed. Random sampling is therefore not involved.

Activity 6

How would you apply cluster sampling to the population referred to in Activity 5?

You would carry out the same procedure to obtain a selected number of postal districts but these districts may be further subdivided so that individual streets are identified. All households of selected streets would then be surveyed.

1.7 *Systematic sampling*

This method can be used with a sampling frame but it is normally used where a sampling frame is not available. The idea is that every *nth* member of a population is selected, where the value of n is determined by the size of the population and by the required sample size. For instance if a 5% sample is to be selected from a population of size 1000, then every 50th person will be selected. The start of the sequence is usually chosen at random. For example, if a 20% sample was to be selected from the student population given in the example, every 5th person would be selected. If you started with, say, the third student, your sample would consist of B. Booth, P. Frome, M. Jones, S. Moore and L. Nupper.

Clearly it would be pointless asking people who hadn't seen the film so your target population will be those people who have recently seen it. The easiest method is to wait outside the cinema and select people as they leave. If there were 300 people watching the film then you need to stop every 30th person.

Systematic sampling is a very quick and efficient method of obtaining a sample. The sample should be random provided there is no pattern in the way people are ordered in the population. For example, if a population consisted of married couples then it is possible for the sample to consist of all husbands or all wives. To illustrate this point the list below refers to records taken from a registry office.

Name	Date of marriage	Nationality
Mr. A. Smith	21/3/93	British
Miss N. Taylor	21/3/93	British
Mr. F. Barker	22/3/93	British
Miss F. Tooch	22/3/93	Australian
Mr. T. Barry	22/3/93	British
Ms. K. Larch	22/3/93	Canadian

If you took a systematic sample that took every second person and you started at F. Barker, all your sample would be males.

1.8 Quota sampling

I am sure that you have seen an interviewer in a town centre with a clip board waiting to pounce on some unsuspecting individual! The interviewer is in fact looking for particular groups of individuals that meet the categories that he or she has been asked to interview. Within each group there will be number or quota of people required and the survey is complete when the quotas have been reached. Quota sampling is a non-probabilistic version of stratified sampling. The quotas within each group should, like stratified sampling, reflect the proportions within the target population.

Your first decision must be the location and time of the survey. An obvious choice would probably be the town centre on a Saturday when many people are out shopping. To reflect the fact that 30% of the population is between 12 and 20 you want a quota of 30 individuals in this age range. Similarly for the other two age bands you would want 60 and 10 individuals respectively.

Quota sampling is a cheap and quick method of obtaining a sample. It is a particularly popular method for market research surveys and opinion polls. Its main disadvantage is that the sample could be heavily biased in favour of one particular group. For instance, in the case of the shopping centre the group of people who do not shop in the town centre will be omitted.

1.9 Summary

This chapter has introduced you to various survey methods. It is generally impractical to question every member of a target population and a sample of this population is selected instead. In order to achieve reliable results a sample should be representative of the target population. Probabilistic sampling methods will give you a representative sample but these methods require the existence of a sampling frame. Non-probabilistic sampling is generally quicker to carry out but is not as reliable. The table below summarises the different methods available.

	Sampling frame available (probabilistic sampling)	*Sampling frame not available (non-probabilistic sampling)*
Population resides in one place	Simple random sampling or systematic sampling	Systematic sampling
Population geographically scattered	Multi-stage sampling	Cluster sampling
Population is defined by categories	Stratified sampling	Quota sampling

1.10 Further reading

Morris, C, *Quantitative Approaches in Business Studies*, Pitman, 1993, Chapter 3

Harper, W, *Statistics, M & E Handbook Series*, Pitman, 1991, Chapter 3.

Booth, D.J, *A First Course in Statistics*, DP Publications, 1992, Chapter 3.

1.11 Exercises

Progress questions

These question have been designed to help you remember the key points in this chapter. The answers to these questions are given in Appendix 1, page 133.

Give the missing word in each case:

1. All the people or things of interest is called a .... population.

2. A subset of the population is called a ....

3. A list of members of the population is called a sampling ....

4. The simplest method of probabilistic sampling is called simple .... sampling.

5. If the sample is not representative of the population you would say that there is .... in the sample.

6. Two or more samples from the same population could give quite different results. This is due to sampling ....

7. .... sampling allows categories within a population to be considered.

8. .... sampling takes every nth member of the population.

Answer TRUE or FALSE

9. A census is when all members of the population are surveyed.

True ☐ False ☐

10. A postal questionnaire is the fastest method of conducting a survey.

True ☐ False ☐

11. Stratified sampling reduces sampling error.

True ☐ False ☐

12. Cluster sampling is used in conjunction with a sampling frame.

True ☐ False ☐

13. Systematic sampling can be both a probabilistic method and a non-probabilistic method.

True ☐ False ☐

Review questions

These questions have been designed to help you check your comprehension of the key points in this chapter. You may wish to look further than this chapter in order to answer them fully. You will find the reading list useful in this respect. You can check the essential elements of your answers by referring to the appropriate section.

14. Describe the essential differences between a sample and a population (Section 1.2)

15. Why does probabilistic sampling require a sampling frame? (Section 1.2)

16. Describe the essential differences between simple random sampling and systematic sampling. (Sections 1.3 and 1.7)

17. When would you use quota sampling? (Section 1.8)

Multiple choice questions

The answers to these will be given in the Lecturers' Supplement.

18. A sample which is chosen such that every member of the population has an equal chance of being selected is called:
    A   a systematic sample
    B   a simple random sample
    C   a cluster sample

19. A correct statement about quota sampling is that:
    A   quota sampling requires random sampling within each quota
    B   quota sampling does not involve any clustering
    C   quota sampling involves some sort of stratification
    D   quota sampling is generally cheaper and more reliable than simple random sampling

20. Raffles are an example of:
    A   simple random sampling
    B   stratified sampling
    C   systematic sampling

21. The most expensive method of collecting data is:
    A   postal questionnaires
    B   telephone interviewing
    C   face-to-face interviewing

22. Multi-stage sampling is used when:
    A   a sampling frame is unavailable
    B   the population is geographically spread out
    C   the population is very large

Practice questions

Answers to these questions will be given in the Lecturers' Supplement.

23. The table below represents a target population.

a) Using the random numbers 2, 9, 4, 3, 6, 7 select a simple random sample of size 3. What is the average age of your sample and what newspapers do they read?

b) Stratify your sample by sex and repeat part (a)

c) If a systematic sample of size 3 was required and the first person chosen was Steve, who would be the second person chosen?

Name	Sex	Age	Newspaper read
Alan	M	23	Guardian
Steve	M	36	Times
Jane	F	47	Mirror
Chris	M	36	Mirror
Julie	F	41	Sun
Stuart	M	37	Mirror
Jill	F	37	Telegraph
John	M	38	Express
Kim	M	48	Sun

24. You have been asked to conduct a survey into people's views of the council tax. What would be the target population and what would be a good sampling frame?

25. A football club want to obtain the views of its supporters to a possible rise in admission charges. They have decided to obtain a simple random sample of

members of the supporters club. Comment on this proposal and suggest alternative target populations and sampling methods.

26. You have been asked to conduct a survey into the attitudes of school leavers to higher education. You intend to carry this out using the face-to-face interview method. How would you obtain your sample?

27. You have been asked to obtain the reaction to the proposal to pedestrianise your local town centre. What survey methods would you use?

Assignment

Answers to this assignment are included in the Lecturers' supplement.

The Channel Tunnel opened in 1994. Before and during the building of the tunnel a great deal of market research was carried out into the market that the tunnel will attract. You are to use the library to research surveys that have been published. Try and discover the sampling methods used and comment on them. What conclusions were reached regarding the viability of the project?

2 Presentation of data

2.1 Introduction

The human brain finds it difficult to make sense of a large quantity of data. However, once the data is properly organised and presented a surprising amount of information can be derived from it. This chapter first discusses the type of data that you may come across and then looks at the best ways of displaying it.

At the end of this chapter you should be able to:

☐ Distinguish between the different types of data

☐ Tabulate data into an ungrouped or grouped frequency table as appropriate

☐ Use diagrams to present the data and draw appropriate conclusions from these diagrams

☐ Distinguish between symmetrical and skewed distributions

2.2 Data classification

Chapter 1 introduced you to the idea of collecting data about some population using samples. The data collected in this case was *primary* data as it is data collected at source. However, data can also be obtained without the necessity of conducting your own survey. There are many government and other publications, such as the Monthly Digest of Statistics from which data can be extracted. Data obtained in this way is called *secondary* data. Secondary data is easier to collect but it is not always in the form you want it or as complete as you would like. There is also the added problem that since you were not involved in its collection you are not able to comment on its accuracy.

If your idea of data is simply lots of numbers then you may be surprised to learn that there several different classifications of data. *Continuous* data is data that is measured on an interval scale such as length or weight. The important point to note about continuous data is that it does not have a precise value. The weight of an item can be measured to any degree of accuracy depending on the measuring device used. *Discrete* data is data that takes on whole values. The obvious example of discrete data is data obtained by counting. However, there are other examples of discrete data such as the cost of an item or shoe size. *Ordinal* data is data that is given a numerical value but only for comparison purposes. An example of this type of data is an assessment score from 1 to 10. Although 10 may be better that 5 it is not necessarily twice as good. *Categorical* data is data that does not have a numerical value and can only placed in a suitable category. An example of this is hair colour or choice of newspaper.

You should have defined (a) as continuous data since height will be measured using either the metric or imperial system. (b) is categorical data since choice will be destination or home/abroad. (c) will be discrete since employees will earn an exact amount such as £182.55. (d) is also discrete since the number can be found by counting. (e) could be either ordinal or categorical. It would be ordinal if you were asked to give a numerical score and categorical if you were simply asked to say whether you liked or disliked the product.

2.3 Tabulation of data

Example 1

A small survey was carried out into the mode of travel to work. The information below relates to a random sample of 20 employed adults.

Person	Mode of travel	Person	Mode of travel
1	car	11	car
2	car	12	bus
3	bus	13	walk
4	car	14	car
5	walk	15	train
6	cycle	16	bus
7	car	17	car
8	cycle	18	cycle
9	bus	19	car
10	train	20	car

Activity 2

How would you classify this data.

This data is categorical since mode of travel does not have a numerical value. This information would be better displayed as a table.

Mode of travel	Frequency	Relative frequency (%)
Car	9	45
Bus	4	20
Cycle	3	15
Walk	2	10
Train	2	10

Frequency is simply the number of times each category appeared. As well as the actual frequency the *relative frequency* has also been quoted. This is simply the frequency expressed as a percentage and is calculated by dividing a frequency by the total frequency and multiplying by 100.

The order in which you write these down is not important although ordering by frequency makes comparison clearer.

Example 2

The following data gives the number of foreign holidays sold by a travel agent over the past four weeks:

Day	No. sold	Day	No. sold
Mon	10	Mon	13
Tues	12	Tues	10
Wed	9	Wed	12
Thurs	10	Thurs	8
Fri	22	Fri	12
Sat	14	Sat	12
Mon	11	Mon	11
Tues	18	Tues	13
Wed	10	Wed	10
Thurs	10	Thurs	14
Fri	11	Fri	13
Sat	9	Sat	12

Activity 3

How would you classify this data and what can you deduce from the figures?

Can the travel agent sell a fraction of a holiday? Assuming that a holiday is a holiday regardless of the duration or the cost then this is clearly discrete data and would have been obtained by counting. By examining the figures you should see that 10 sales occurs most frequently although there is a range from 8 to 22 sales. To enable this information to be seen more clearly you could aggregate the data into a table as follows:

Number sold	Frequency
8	1
9	2
10	6
11	3
12	5
13	3
14	2
More than 14	2

This table is called an *ungrouped frequency* table since all numbers have been included. This table is a useful way of summarising a small set of discrete data. There are two extreme values or *outliers* of value 18 and 22 sales and these have been included by the use of a 'more than' quantity. From this table you can see that between 10 to 12 holidays are usually sold each day.

Example 3

Table 1 gives the number of bolts produced by a machine each hour over the past 65 hours while table 2 gives the length in mm of 80 of these bolts.

Table 1	*Table 2*
184 250 136 178	49.9 53.8 61.3 45.8
231 158 197 159	51.2 44.5 55.3 51.4
141 218 223 156	84.1 55.7 52.7 68.7
124 177 298 175	52.5 58.8 37.8 44.1
231 218 117 149	49.9 53.8 64.1 35.9
169 119 174	56.4 55.1 60.6 45.9
171 191 202	54.8 54.0 49.3 46.8
214 138 127	46.5 52.2 33.3 42.9
254 177 181	47.7 56.2 40.5 36.8
189 201 198	47.5 56.3 70.2 35.5
165 140 100	56.7 56.0 56.5 49.5
147 188 296	57.5 52.0 36.8 46.3
237 223 267	42.4 30.2 49.5 36.3
147 112 238	54.6 45.1 30.0 47.0
139 165 125	52.1 53.0 66.1 50.5
165 188 230	56.0 50.9 42.7 42.1
150 127 251	51.2 49.0 49.9 54.4
182 139 159	53.2 43.0 41.3 49.7
179 230 183	42.9 61.1 41.7 35.7
166 163 194	45.0 59.2 60.6 44.7

Activity 4

Look at the data in both these tables. Can you deduce anything about how many bolts are produced each hour or the length of each bolt? Would it help if ungrouped frequency tables were created as in Activity 2?

I expect that you found it quite difficult to draw many conclusions from the data. For table 1 you might have identified the range of production as between 100 to 298 bolts per hour but what is the 'normal' production rate? Similarly, the smallest bolt is 30.0 mm and the largest is 84.1 mm but what size are the majority of the bolts? An ungrouped frequency table for either set of data would not be very helpful for two reasons. For both data sets the range of the data is large, which would necessitate a large table and for table 2 the data is continuous. Continuous data, can by definition, take on any value so what values would you use in your table? To overcome these problems a *grouped frequency table* is produced. A grouped frequency table is similar to an ungrouped table except that intervals are set up into which the data can be grouped. The number and size of each interval depends on the quantity and range of your data. In general you would have between 8 to 15 intervals and the width of each interval, or the *class interval* should be a convenient number such as 10, 20, 25 etc. In the case of table 1 the range is 298 − 100 = 198 and a class interval of 20 would give you 10 intervals, which is about right. The first interval would be 100 to 119, the second 120 to 139 and so on. Once you have decided on the size of each interval you need to allocate each value to one of the intervals. This can be done by using a *tally chart*. A tally chart is simply a foolproof means (or nearly) of ensuring that all items have been allocated. You start with the first value, in this case 184, and find the relevant interval, which is 180 to 199. A '1' is placed in this row. You then do the same with subsequent values, except that when you have four 1's in a row you would draw a line through the group to make the total of 5. This has been done for you in the chart below.

Class interval	Tally
100 to 119	1111
120 to 139	1111 111
140 to 159	1111 1111
160 to 179	1111 1111 111
180 to 199	1111 1111 1
200 to 219	1111
220 to 239	1111 111
240 to 259	111
260 to 279	1
280 to 299	11

The next stage is to add up the tally in each interval to give you the frequency. The final grouped frequency table is as shown on the following page.

Interval	Frequency	Relative frequency (%)
100 to 119	4	6.2
120 to 139	8	12.3
140 to 159	10	15.4
160 to 179	13	20.0
180 to 199	11	16.9
200 to 219	5	7.7
220 to 239	8	12.3
240 to 259	3	4.6
260 to 279	1	1.5
280 to 299	2	3.1
Total	65	100

From this table it appears that the rate of production is quite variable although the rate is unlikely to be less than 120 or more than 240 bolts per hour.

How would you group the data in table 2? You might decide on a class interval of 5mm, which would give you 11 intervals. Since the smallest length is 30mm the first group would start at 30mm, the second at 35mm and so on. But what should the end of each group be? If you used 34mm you would not be able to allocate a value between 34 and 35mm. You cannot use the same figure for both the end of one group and the start of the next because this would allow a value to be added to more than one group. It is essential that a value can go into *one and only one* interval so the ranges must be designed to guarantee this. Since the data is continuous the length can be quoted to any degree of accuracy so the end of each group would be defined as *under* 35mm and under 40mm and so on. In this way a length of 34.9mm would be in the first group while 35.0mm would be in the second group.

Activity 5

Obtain the grouped frequency table for the data in table 2 of Example 3. What can you deduce about the length of bolts produced.

You should have obtained the following table (shown on the following page).

Interval	Frequency	Relative frequency (%)
30 to under 35mm	3	3.75
35 to under 40mm	7	8.75
40 to under 45mm	12	15.00
45 to under 50mm	18	22.50
50 to under 55mm	18	22.50
55 to under 60mm	13	16.25
60 to under 65mm	5	6.25
65 to under 70mm	2	2.50
70 to under 75mm	1	1.25
75 to under 80mm	0	0
80 to under 85mm	1	1.25

If you look at this table the *distribution* of the lengths are clearer. 76% of the values are between 40 to 60mm with few over 60mm or less than 40mm.

In both these examples the class intervals were the same for the whole distribution, that is 20 in the first case and 5 in the second. However, it is not necessary for the intervals to be equal and you may have two or more different intervals in the same table. In the length data you might decide to condense the last three intervals into one since the frequencies in these intervals are small. If you do this your last interval will be 70 to under 85mm, which has a frequency of 2. It is also possible to have an open interval at the beginning or end such as greater than 70mm or less than 30mm. However, only use open intervals if you really have to and only if there is a relatively small number of items in this interval.

Example 4

The table below has been taken from The Monthly Digest of Statistics (with permission).

8.1 Inland energy consumption: primary fuel input basis

Million tonnes of oil or oil equivalent

		Not seasonally adjusted						Seasonally adjusted (annual rates)[7]						
					Primary electricity							Primary electricity		
		Coal[1]	Petro-leum[2]	Natural gas[3]	Nuclear	Natural flow hydro[5]	Net imports	Total	Coal[1,4]	Petro-leum[2,4]	Natural gas[3,4]	Nuclear	Natural flow hydro[5]	Net imports[6]	Total
		BHBB	BHBC	BHBD	BHBE	BHBF	BHBM	BHBA	BHBH	BHBI	BHBJ	BHBK	BHBL	BHBN	BHBG
1987		68.3	64.3	50.5	11.7	1.2	2.8	198.9	67.2	63.5	49.6	11.7	1.2	2.8	196.1
1988		65.9	68.3	47.9	13.5	1.4	3.1	200.1	65.9	68.3	49.7	13.5	1.4	3.1	201.9
1989		63.6	69.5	47.4	15.4	1.4	3.0	200.2	64.5	70.2	50.5	15.4	1.4	3.0	204.9
1990		63.8	71.3	49.0	14.2	1.6	2.9	202.7	65.0	73.3	52.4	14.2	1.6	2.9	209.3
1991		63.3	71.1	52.8	15.2	1.4	3.9	207.7	63.1	70.8	52.7	15.2	1.4	3.9	207.0
1992	Aug	3.7	5.1	1.9	1.2	0.1	0.3	12.2	58.5	68.4	55.8	15.4	1.50	4.0	203.5
	Sep	5.0	7.0	3.3	1.5	0.2	0.4	17.2	56.7	74.8	57.2	16.9	1.60	4.1	211.3
	Oct	4.6	5.4	4.2	1.2	0.1	0.3	15.9	59.4	68.4	55.1	15.2	1.50	4.1	203.8
	Nov	4.9	5.5	5.5	1.3	0.1	0.3	17.6	58.7	70.0	54.5	17.5	1.50	4.1	206.3
	Dec	5.9	7.1	7.5	1.9	0.2	0.4	23.0	54.6	65.9	54.6	19.3	1.60	4.1	200.1
1993	Jan	4.5	5.2	6.3	1.6	0.2	0.3	18.7	51.6	69.6	57.9	17.4	1.50	4.1	202.3
	Feb	4.9	5.6	6.7	1.7	0.1	0.3	19.4	53.2	68.5	59.5	17.3	1.50	4.1	204.1
	Mar	5.7	6.8	6.6	1.9	0.1	0.4	21.7	54.6	70.3	53.6	19.9	1.40	4.1	204.0
	Apr	3.8	5.2	4.3	1.5	0.1	0.3	15.3	51.1	71.3	56.7	20.1	1.40	4.1	204.8
	May	3.8	5.1	3.5	1.3	0.1	0.3	14.0	53.3	68.6	58.2	16.0	1.40	4.1	201.6
	Jun	4.1	6.6	3.2	1.7	0.1	0.3	16.0	50.2	72.8	60.0	22.3	1.40	3.4	210.3
	Jul	3.4	5.3	2.5	1.3	0.1	0.3	12.8	49.2	70.2	60.4	21.0	1.50	3.6	205.9
	Aug	3.4	5.2	2.7	1.3	0.1	0.3	12.9	51.7	70.1	59.1	18.4	1.50	4.0	207.3
	Sep	4.2	7.0	4.0	1.8	0.1	0.4	17.5	47.5	68.3	63.3	20.8	1.40	4.1	205.5
	Oct	4.0	5.5	5.1	1.5	0.1	0.3	16.6	49.5	68.9	65.0	21.2	1.37	4.2	206.3

1 Consumption by fuel producers plus disposals (including imports) to final users plus (for annual unadjusted figures only) net foreign trade and stock change in other solid fuels. See also footnotes 6 and 7 to Table 8.4.
2 Inland deliveries for energy use plus refinery fuel and losses minus the difference between deliveries to and actual consumption at power stations and gasworks.
3 Including non-energy use and excluding gas fired or re-injected.
4 Also temperature corrected.
5 Excludes generation from pumped storage stations. Includes generation at wind stations.
6 Not seasonally adjusted.
7 For hydro the estimated annual out-turn.

Source: Department of Trade and Industry.

This table is an example of secondary data since the data has been compiled for you. Energy consumption has been allocated to specific categories so this data can be treated as categorical with the consumption figures used as frequencies. A casual glance at this data suggests that coal, petroleum and gas make up the bulk of the energy consumed in the U.K and that there appears to be some variation between months. You will now see that more information can be obtained from this data by the use of diagrams.

2.4 Diagrammatic representation of data

Although frequency tables can give you more information than the raw data, it can still be difficult to take in all the information that is inherent in the data. Diagrams can help provide this additional information and also display the data in a more visually attractive manner. You do lose some detail but this is a small price to pay for the additional information that diagrams provide. There are several types of diagrams and the choice depends mainly on the type of data but also on your intended audience.

2.4.1 Pie charts

When you want to compare the relative sizes of the frequencies a pie chart is a good choice of diagram. It is normally used for categorical data and each category is represented by a segment of a circle. The size of each segment reflects the frequency of that category and can be represented as an angle. For example, 45% of the sample in Example 1 travelled by car so a segment with an angle of 45% of 360° (= 162°) could be used to represent this category. An easy way to calculate the angle is to multiply the percentage frequency by 3.6. For example 45 × 3.6 = 162.

The angles are shown below.

Mode of travel	Frequency	Relative frequency	Angle
Car	9	45%	162°
Bus	4	20%	72°
Cycle	3	15%	54°
Walk	2	10%	36°
Train	2	10%	36°

The pie chart for this data is shown in Figure 1 below.

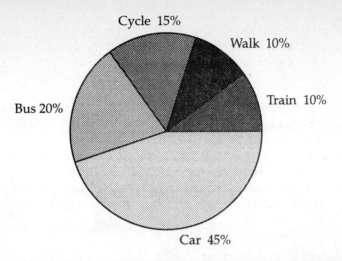

Figure 1 Pie chart

2.4.2 Bar charts

A pie chart is useful for showing the relative sizes of each category and is visually appealing but it is more difficult to draw than some diagrams. It is also limited in the information that it can display. A *simple bar chart* is another useful method of displaying categorical data, or an ungrouped frequency table. For each category a vertical bar is drawn, the *height* of the bar being proportional to the frequency. The diagram below shows the mode of transport data in the form of a simple bar chart.

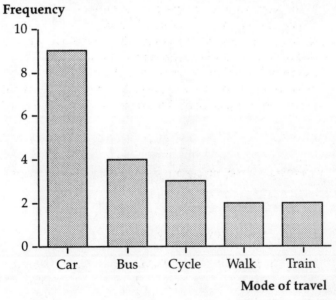

Figure 2 Simple bar chart

Sometimes a category can be subdivided into several sub-categories or components. In these cases there are two other forms of a bar chart that can be used to display and compare the data. If you are interested in comparing totals and seeing how the totals are made up a *component* bar chart is used. Figure 3 is a component bar chart for the data displayed in Example 4. In this figure you can see the variation in total consumption for month to month. You can also see the relative sizes of the individual fuels.

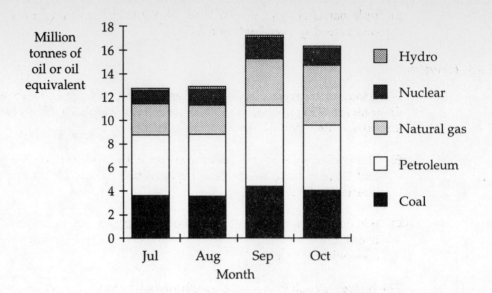

Figure 3 Component bar chart

A *multiple bar chart* is used when you are interested in changes in the components but the totals are of no interest. Figure 4 below is a multiple bar chart for the fuel example.

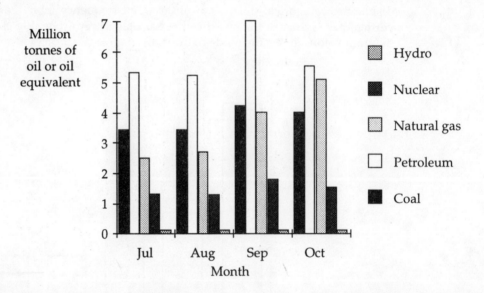

Figure 4 Multiple bar chart

Activity 8

What can you conclude about the energy consumption from both diagrams?

You should have deduced from the component bar chart that the total energy consumption was highest in September. Petroleum is the largest proportion of the 5 fuels and this can be seen from both charts. It is also clear from the component bar chart that hydroelectric power adds a negligible amount to the total. From the multiple bar chart you should have seen that the consumption of natural gas has increased steadily over the 4 months.

2.4.3 Histograms

For grouped frequency tables a different type of diagram is normally used. This diagram is called a histogram and although it may look like a bar chart there are some important differences. These are:

■ The horizontal axis is a continuous scale, just like a normal graph. This implies that there should not be gaps between bars unless the frequency for that class interval really is zero.

■ It is the area of the bars that are being compared, not the heights. This means that if one class interval is twice the others then the height must be halved since area=width × height.

The histogram below is for the lengths of bolts given in Example 3 and uses an equal class interval of 5mm.

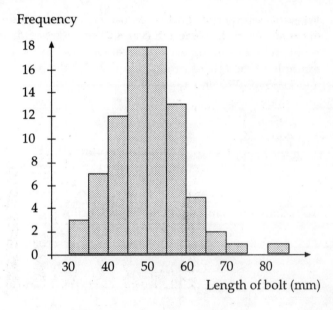

Figure 5 Histogram

If the last three intervals were combined the last class interval would be 15mm. In this case the frequency of 2 should be *divided* by 3 to give 0.67 and the histogram would have to be redrawn as shown in Figure 6 below.

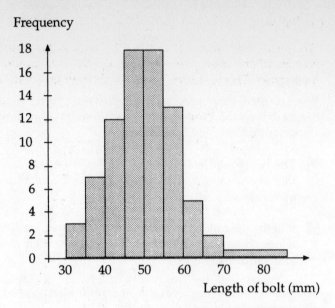

Figure 6 Histogram- unequal class intervals

When you draw histograms for discrete data there is a problem in that there is a gap between the end of one interval and the start of the next. You can get around this problem by extending each interval half way to the next or last interval. Thus for the example of the rate of production of bolts, the intervals would become 100.5 to 119.5 and 119.5 to 139.5 and so on.

Activity 9

Draw the histogram for the production rate data.

Your diagram should look like the one below:

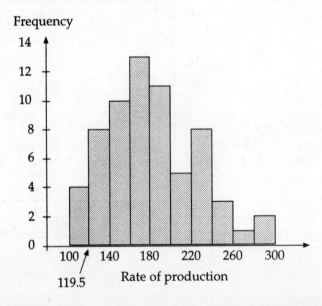

Figure 7 Histogram for discrete data

2.4.4 *Frequency Polygons*

To get a better idea about how the data is distributed across the range of possible values of the data, you can join up the mid points of the top of each bar of the histogram. This is shown below for the bolt length data.

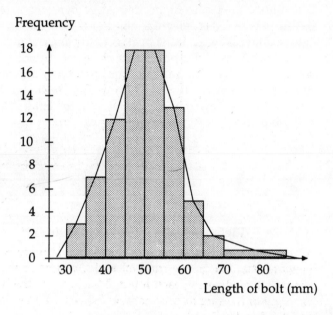

Figure 8

If the bars are now removed, you are left with a picture of the shape of the underlying distribution of the data. The area under the frequency polygon is the same as the area under the original histogram.

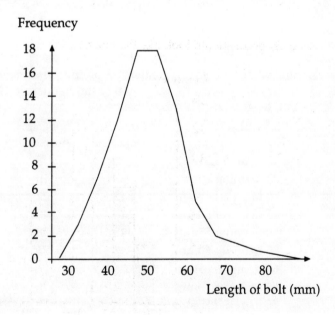

Figure 9 Frequency polygon

25

This diagram can be quite useful if you want to compare different distributions as it is possible to plot more than one frequency polygon on the same graph. This is not possible with the other diagrams you have met as they would look too confusing.

Another important use of the frequency polygon is to categorise the shape of the distribution in terms of its degree of symmetry. A distribution that is perfectly balanced is called *symmetrical* whereas a distribution which has its peak offset to one side is called skewed. If the peak is to the left, the distribution is called *right or positive skewed*, whereas if the peak is to the right, the distribution is called *left or negative skewed*. This may sound illogical but you will discover the reason for this convention in the next chapter. I find it easier to look at the tail of the distribution. If it is to the right it is right skewed and if the tail is to the left it is left skewed. The diagrams below may help you appreciate the differences

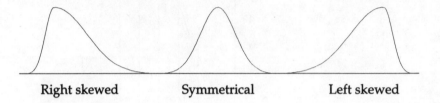

| Right skewed | Symmetrical | Left skewed |

Figure 10

Activity 10

How would you define the shape of the distribution of bolt lengths?

The distribution is approximately symmetrical although it has a slight right skewness to it.

2.4.5 Cumulative frequency ogive

Another diagram can be created by plotting the *cumulative* frequencies. Cumulative frequency is simply a running total of the frequencies. The cumulative frequencies for the bolt length data are shown below.

Interval	Frequency frequency	Cumulative frequency	% cumulative frequency
30 to under 35mm	3	3	3.75
35 to under 40mm	7	10	12.50
40 to under 45mm	12	22	27.50
45 to under 50mm	18	40	50.00
50 to under 55mm	18	58	72.50
55 to under 60mm	13	71	88.75
60 to under 65mm	5	76	95.00
65 to under 70mm	2	78	97.50
70 to under 75mm	1	79	98.75
75 to under 80mm	0	79	98.75
80 to under 85mm	1	80	100.00

The percentage cumulative frequencies have also been calculated as you will find that the use of percentages has certain advantages. The cumulative frequency graph or *ogive* can now be drawn. The *upper* boundaries of each class interval are plotted against the (%) cumulative frequencies as shown below.

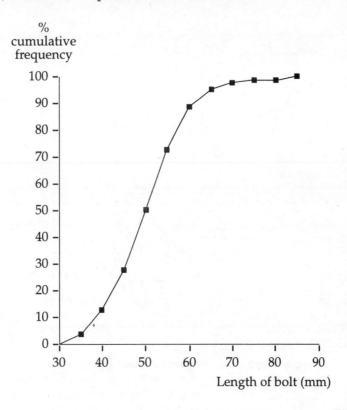

Figure 11 Ogive

This is a very useful diagram and you will meet this again in the next chapter. For the purposes of this chapter you can treat this graph as a *less than* graph since the upper class boundaries were plotted against the cumulative frequencies. So, for example, 12.5% of the lengths are below 40mm.

Activity 11

Determine the proportion of lengths that are:

a) below 50mm

b) below 41mm

c) above 63mm

The answer to (a) can be read directly from the grouped frequency distribution and is 50%. However, for both (b) and (c) you should use the ogive to *interpolate* between two boundaries. To do this you should draw a vertical line up from the X axis at the appropriate value to meet the ogive. You can then draw a horizontal line from this point until it meets the Y axis and then it is a matter of reading the cumulative frequency from this axis. This has been done for you in Figure 12 below.

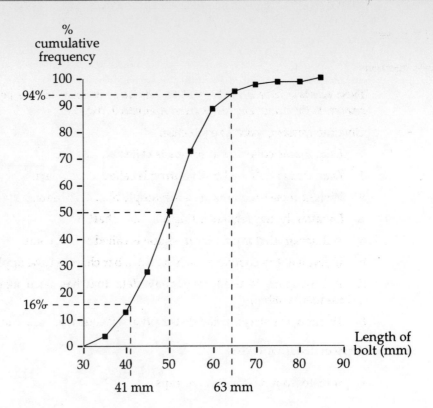

Figure 12

You will see from the diagram that I have drawn lines for all three lengths. The cumulative frequency for (a) is 50% as it should be. The cumulative frequency for (b) is approximately 16% so 16% of lengths are below 41mm. The cumulative frequency for (c) is approximately 94% but as you were asked to find the proportion above 63mm then you need to subtract 94 from 100, that is 6%.

2.5 Summary

This chapter has enabled you to understand the importance of tabulating and presenting data. Data can be continuous, discrete, ordinal or categorical and the type of data determines the method to use for its presentation. Data is normally aggregated into tables and for continuous and discrete data these tables can be either ungrouped or grouped. For group frequency tables the class interval needs to be decided and a tally chart used to help in the aggregation process. There are several different types of diagram that can be used to display the data more effectively. Pie charts and bar charts can be used for categorical data, ordinal data and for ungrouped discrete data. Histograms are used for either continuous or discrete data that has been aggregated into a frequency table. A histogram gives you an idea of the shape of the underlying distribution but a frequency polygon will show this more clearly. If cumulative frequencies are plotted, a cumulative frequency ogive is obtained and this important graph allows you to obtain further information about the distribution.

2.6 Further reading

Morris, C, *Quantitative Approaches in Business Studies*, Pitman, 1993, Chapter 5

Harper, W, *Statistics, M & E Handbook Series*, Pitman, 1991, Chapter 6.

Francis, A. *Business Mathematics and Statistics*, DP Publications, Chapter 4.

2.7 Exercises

Progress questions

These question have been designed to help you remember the key points in this chapter. The answers to these questions are given in Appendix 1, page 133.

Give the missing word in each case:

1. Data that is collected at source is called.......... data.

2. Data that is obtained by counting is called............ data.

3. Weight measurements are an example of.............. data.

4. Data can be aggregated using a............. chart.

5. A diagram that is circular in shape is called a......... chart.

6. If you want to compare totals a............ bar chart may be applicable.

7. A histogram is used to display data that has been aggregated into a............ frequency table.

8. To show the shape of the distribution a frequency........... can be used.

Answer TRUE or FALSE

9. A histogram must not have gaps.

    True ☐ False ☐

10. A histogram compares heights of each bar.

    True ☐ False ☐

11. The upper end of each interval should be plotted for a cumulative frequency ogive.

    True ☐ False ☐

12. A survey into types of heating found in domestic property would form a set of discrete data.

    True ☐ False ☐

13. Data is aggregated into a grouped frequency table if the quantity of data is very large.

    True ☐ False ☐

14. Data obtained from a survey into the occupancy of cars could be displayed by a pie chart.

    True ☐ False ☐

Review questions

These questions have been designed to help you check your comprehension of the key points in this chapter. You may wish to look further than this chapter in order to answer them fully. You will find the reading list useful in this respect. You can check the essential elements of your answers by referring to the appropriate section.

15. What is the difference between a grouped and ungrouped frequency distribution? (Section 2.3)

16. Describe the essential differences between a bar chart and a histogram (Section 2.4)

17. What are the uses of a frequency polygon? (Section 2.4.4)

18. What would the distribution of wages earned by the working population of Britain look like? (Section 2.4.4)

19. What is a cumulative frequency ogive? (Section 2.4.5)

Multiple choice questions

The answers to these will be given in the Lecturers' Supplement.

20. The graph of a cumulative frequency distribution is called:
    A   a line graph
    B   a histogram
    C   an Ogive

21. The difference between a Histogram and a Bar Chart is:
    A   A histogram represent the frequency whereas a bar chart represents the number.
    B   With a histogram areas represent frequencies, whereas with a bar chart heights represents frequencies.
    C   Histograms are used for comparing categorical data.

22. Categorical data is data that:
    A   Is obtained by measurement.
    B   Is obtained by counting.
    C   does not have a numerical value.

23. A multiple bar chart is used to compare:
    A   Totals
    B   Changes to components
    C   Grouped data

24. A frequency polygon is used in conjunction with a:
    A   A simple bar chart
    B   A component bar chart
    C   A multiple bar chart
    D   Histogram

25. A frequency distribution that has its peak to the left is called:
    A   Left skewed
    B   Symmetrical
    C   Right skewed

Practice questions

Answers to these questions will be given in the Lecturers' Supplement.

26. How would you define the following sets of data?
    a)   The number of hours of sunshine each day at a seaside resort.
    b)   The mean daily temperature at a seaside resort
    c)   Daily rainfall (in mm)
    d)   Scoring system for ice dancing

27. A survey was carried out into consumer's preference for different types of coffee. A sample of 20 people gave the following replies:

Person	Preference	Person	Preference
1	instant	11	ground
2	filter	12	instant
3	instant	13	ground
4	filter	14	filter
5	instant	15	instant
6	filter	16	instant
7	ground	17	ground
8	instant	18	filter
9	filter	19	instant
10	filter	20	filter

a) Aggregate this data into a suitable table.
b) Draw a pie chart of the data.
c) Draw a simple bar chart of the data.

28. The following table represents the sales by department of a high street store.

Department	1991	1992	1993
Menswear	£2.7m	£4.9m	£6.3m
Furniture	£3.4m	£2.3m	£2.4m
Household	£2.5m	£2.4m	£2.5m
Total Sales	£8.6m	£9.6m	£10.3m

Draw a component bar chart and a multiple bar chart of the sales. What conclusions can you make about the sales for this store?

29. The following table shows how the sales of Marla plc were broken down between the company's four sales regions during the years 1989 to 1993.

Sales Region	Year (Sales £m)				
	1989	1990	1991	1992	1993
S. West	4.0	2.0	2.2	3.6	3.7
South	6.0	4.9	2.5	3.2	3.7
S. East	7.6	9.1	5.2	4.3	4.2
Wales	1.5	1.4	1.4	1.5	1.6
Totals	19.1	17.4	11.3	12.6	13.2

a) Draw a simple bar chart to show the total sales for the four year period;
b) Draw a component bar chart to show the sales for the years and how they were broken down between the four sales regions;
c) Draw a multiple bar chart to compare the sales for each region.
d) Draw a pie chart to show the breakdown of total sales in 1993.
e) What can you conclude about the sales of Marla plc?

30. The data below relates to the weight (in grams) of an item produced by a machine.

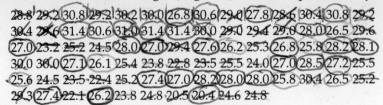

28.8 29.2 30.8 29.2 30.2 30.0 26.8 30.6 29.0 27.8 28.6 30.4 30.8 29.2
30.4 28.6 31.4 30.6 31.0 31.4 31.4 30.0 29.0 29.4 29.0 28.0 26.5 29.6
27.0 23.2 25.2 24.5 28.0 27.0 29.4 27.6 26.2 25.3 26.8 25.8 28.2 28.1
30.0 30.0 27.1 26.1 25.4 23.8 22.8 23.5 25.5 24.0 27.0 28.5 27.2 25.5
25.6 24.5 23.5 22.4 25.2 27.4 27.0 28.2 28.0 28.0 25.8 30.4 26.5 25.2
29.3 27.4 22.1 26.2 23.8 24.8 20.5 20.4 24.6 24.8

a) Aggregate this data into a suitable frequency table.

b) Draw a histogram of the data.

c) Draw a frequency polygon of the data.

d) Draw a cumulative frequency ogive of the data and demonstrate how it could be used to provide further information about the distribution of weights.

e) What conclusions can be made about the data from your diagrams?

31. The sickness records of a company have been examined and the table below shows the number of days taken off work through sickness during the past year.

Days off work	Number of employees
Less than 2 days	45
2 to 5 days	89
6 to 9 days	40
10 to 13 days	25
14 to 21 days	5
22 to 29 days	2

Draw a histogram to represent this distribution and comment on its shape.

Assignment

Answers to this assignment are included in the Lecturers' supplement.

The table below has been taken from Economic Trends. Examine this table and use appropriate diagrams in order to draw conclusions regarding the way that expenditure was proportioned between categories for 1992. Is there any indication that this proportion varies with season of the year?

5 Real consumers' expenditure – component categories

£ million, 1990 prices

		Durable goods	Food	Alcoholic drink and tobacco	Clothing and footwear	Energy products	Other goods	Rent, rates and water charges	Other services[1]	total+
		CCBW	CCCA	FCCD	FCCE	CCCG	CCCM	CCCN	CCCJ	CAAB
1989		36 815	42 281	30 433	20 662	22 305	38 485	38 426	115 999	345 406
1990		34 745	41 816	30 272	20 876	22 422	39 566	38 915	118 915	347 527
1991		30 472	41 870	29 437	20 535	23 209	38 563	39 328	116 579	339 993
1992		30 752	42 380	28 667	20 629	22 977	38 873	38 682	115 981	339 941
1989	Q2	9 432	10 653	7 652	5 190	5 716	9 522	9 590	28 717	86 472
	Q3	9 099	10 508	7 590	5 095	5 543	9 631	9 616	29 161	86 243
	Q4	9 120	10 525	7 565	5 123	5 708	9 850	9 651	29 302	86 844
1990	Q1	9 054	10 479	7 572	5 325	5 414	9 940	9 679	29 529	86 992
	Q2	8 872	10 521	7 603	5 298	5 641	9 911	9 713	29 850	87 409
	Q3	8 561	10 369	7 573	5 236	5 742	9 876	9 747	29 674	86 778
	Q4	8 258	10 447	7 524	5 017	5 625	9 839	9 776	29 862	86 348
1991	Q1	7 933	10 459	7 472	5 186	5 775	9 733	9 799	29 477	85 834
	Q2	7 491	10 443	7 285	5 121	5 985	9 598	9 820	29 063	84 806
	Q3	7 670	10 478	7 394	5 145	5 637	9 638	9 842	28 908	84 712
	Q4	7 378	10 490	7 286	5 083	5 812	9 594	9 867	29 131	84 641
1992	Q1	7 452	10 453	7 204	5 000	5 656	9 578	9 890	29 044	84 277
	Q2	7 552	10 598	7 266	5 116	5 612	9 761	9 908	29 025	84 838
	Q3	7 768	10 621	7 085	5 190	5 806	9 787	9 930	28 997	85 184
	Q4	7 980	10 708	7 112	5 323	5 903	9 747	9 954	28 915	85 642
1993	Q1	8 046	10 753	7 124	5 298	5 649	9 943	9 978	29 080	85 871
	Q2	8 157	10 651	7 164	5 316	5 703	10 024	9 996	29 169	86 180

1 Including the adjustments for international travel, etc. and final expenditure by private non-profit-making bodies.

Source: Central Statistical Office

3 Summarising data

3.1 Introduction

Although tables and diagrams allow important features of data to be displayed, these methods of summarising the information are generally qualitative rather than quantitative. In order to provide more quantitative information it is necessary to calculate statistical measures that can be used to represent the entire set of data. Two important measures of the data are the location of the data in terms of a typical or central value and the spread or dispersion of the data around this central value. To successfully complete this chapter you should have worked through Chapter 2 (Presentation of data).

At the end of this chapter you should be able to:

❑ Calculate the mean, median and mode for small sets of data and also for frequency distributions.

❑ Understand the advantages and disadvantages of each type of average.

❑ Understand the need for measures of spread and to be able to use the cumulative frequency ogive to find the interquartile range.

❑ Calculate the standard deviation for small sets of data and for frequency distributions.

❑ Draw and use box and whisker plots.

3.2 Measures of location

I am sure that you all have heard of the word 'average'. An average is some kind of representative item within a set of possible items. The word location is used because for numerical data, an average 'locates' a typical value of some distribution. This is as not as easy as it may seem as there could be several different values that would serve as this average figure.

Example 1

The number of sales made by two sales persons over the past few days has been as follows:

	Sales per day
Mike:	3, 2, 1, 32, 2, 1, 1
Janet:	0, 1, 4, 12, 10, 7, 8, 6

Activity 1

What would be a good measure of the number of sales by each sales person?

Six out of the seven values for Mike are between 1 and 3 sales, while for Janet the values are fairly evenly spread between 0 and 12 sales. Do you choose one of the existing values to represent the number of sales or do you choose a value that is in between?

There are in fact three different averages and each can give you a different value. The next section defines each one and discusses the advantages and disadvantages of each.

3.2.1 The mean, median and mode

The mean is defined as the sum of all the values divided by the total number of values. So for Mike the mean number of sales is:

$$\frac{3+2+1+3+2+1+1}{7} = 6$$

Notice that the mean is a not one of the values in the set of data. (A mean value can also be a fractional value even if the data values are themselves whole numbers).

The mean of a set of numbers is normally referred to as $\bar{x}$ (x bar) and in symbols the formula for the mean is:

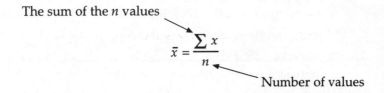

The sum of the n values

$$\bar{x} = \frac{\sum x}{n}$$

Number of values

Activity 2

Find the mean number of sales for Janet?

You should have found that the mean for Janet is also 6. Is 6 sales a good measure of average for both data sets? Certainly for Janet a mean of 6 is quite a good representative value but for Mike a value between 1 and 3 would be more typical. The problem with the mean is that it gives equal importance to *all* values, including any extreme values. In Mike's case the value of 32 is clearly influencing the mean. The *median* overcomes this problem by choosing the *middle* value of a set of numbers. In order to find this value the data is first ordered in ascending order as follows:

$$1, 1, 1, 2, 2, 3, 32$$

The middle value of this set of 7 numbers is 2, which is a more typical value.

Activity 3

Find the median sales for Janet.

You should have found a slight problem here in that there is no single middle number. There are two middle numbers though, which are 6 and 7 and in this case you would take the mean of these two numbers which is 6.5. This is close to the mean value of 6, so in this case either of the two averages are equally suitable.

Which is the better average? This is a difficult question to answer as both have their advantages and disadvantages as you can see in the table below.

	Mean	Median
One of the actual data items?	Not usually	Usually
Equal contribution by all data items?	Yes	No
Influenced by extreme values (outliers)?	Yes	No
Easy to calculate?	Yes	No

The mean and median can both be used for numerical data but not for *categorical* data. The next activity illustrates this point.

Activity 4

In chapter 2, page 15, data was provided into a travel to work survey. This data is summarised in the table below.

Mode of travel	Frequency
Car	9
Bus	4
Cycle	3
Walk	2
Train	2

Which is the most typical mode of travel

Clearly the car is the most common mode of travel. The category that occurs the most frequently is called the *mode*. The mode can also be quoted for numerical data.

Activity 5

What is the mode for the sales data of Example 1?

For Mike, 1 sale occurred most frequently so this is the mode for this group of numbers. However, there is no mode for Janet's sales data since each value occurs once only.

The mode has limited uses but it can be useful when the most common value or category is required. Can you imagine a shoe shop being interested in the mean or median size of shoe?

3.2.2 The mean, median and mode for a frequency distribution

It is relatively straightforward finding an average of a small set of data. But when large quantities of data are involved or when the data is supplied in the form of a frequency table, the methods of calculation become more involved.

Example 2

The ungrouped frequency table below gives the daily number of sales made by the sales force of a double glazing company.

No. of sales	Frequency
2	3
3	7
4	9
5	6
6	5
7	2
8	1

Activity 6

What is the mean number of sales made per day by the company's sales force?

The mean could be found by writing the value 2 three times, 3 seven times and so on. You would then add up all the values and divide by the total number of values, which is 33. However, a much easier method is to multiply 2 by 3, 3 by 7 and so on. This will give you the same sum as using the longer method. If you let 'x' be the number of sales and 'f' the frequency the procedure for calculating the mean can be seen below.

No. of sales x	Frequency f	fx
2	3	6
3	7	21
4	9	36
5	6	30
6	5	30
7	2	14
8	1	8
Total	33	145

The mean is therefore: $\dfrac{145}{33} = 4.4$ sales.

This calculation can be expressed in algebraic notation as follows:

Multiply f by x and sum

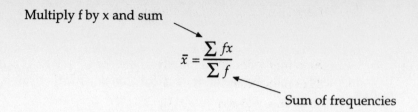

$$\bar{x} = \frac{\sum fx}{\sum f}$$

Sum of frequencies

Activity 7

What is the median number of sales made per day?

The median for this set of values can be found by remembering that the median is the middle value. Since the data is already in ascending order it is a simple matter of locating the middle value, which will occur at the 17th frequency. If you write down the cumulative frequencies as shown below you will see that the median must occur when $x = 4$.

x	f	Cumulative f
2	3	3
3	7	10
4	9	19
5	6	25
6	5	30
7	2	32
8	1	33

Activity 8

What is the modal value of sales?

The modal number of sales is easy to see since 4 sales occurs 9 times which is the most frequent.

Example 3

The group frequency table below refers to the length of 80 bolts produced by a machine.

Interval	Frequency
30 to under 35mm	3
35 to under 40mm	7
40 to under 45mm	12
45 to under 50mm	18
50 to under 55mm	18
55 to under 60mm	13
60 to under 65mm	5
65 to under 70mm	2
70 to under 75mm	1
75 to under 80mm	0
80 to under 85mm	1

This is a similar table to Example 2 except that 'x' does not have a single value. In order to calculate the mean the mid value is used for x. So the *mid value* for the interval 30 to under 35 would be 32.5mm. (You can assume that you can get as close as you like to 35mm). Although this is an approximation it is generally a very close one and is normally quite adequate.

Activity 9

Calculate the mean for the data in Example 3.

Using the mid point to represent 'x' the table in Example 3 becomes:

Interval	x	x^2	f	fx	fx^2
30 to under 35mm	32.5	1056·25	3	97.5	3168·75
35 to under 40mm	37.5	1406·25	7	262.5	9843·75
40 to under 45mm	42.5	1806·25	12	510.0	21675
45 to under 50mm	47.5	2256·25	18	855.0	40612·5
50 to under 55mm	52.5	2756·25	18	945.0	49612·5
55 to under 60mm	57.5	3306·25	13	747.5	42981·25
60 to under 65mm	62.5	3906·25	5	312.5	19531·25
65 to under 70mm	67.5	4556·25	2	135.0	9112·5
70 to under 75mm	72.5	5256·25	1	72.5	5256·25
75 to under 80mm	77.5	6006·25	0	0.0	0
80 to under 85mm	82.5	6806·25	1	82.5	6806·25
Total			80	4020	

and the mean is:

$$\frac{4020}{80} = 50.25 \text{ mm}$$

The mean using the raw data is 50.03mm, so the value obtained using the frequency table is quite a good one. (If you want the check this calculation the raw data can be found in Example 3 of Chapter 2).

The problem with obtaining the median from a grouped frequency table is that the median is likely to lie within an interval. You could locate the required interval and then simply use the mid point as an estimate but a better a better approximation is to *interpolate* within the interval. The easiest method is graphical and if a cumulative frequency ogive is drawn the median frequency will be *half* way up the Y axis. It is often easier to use percentage cumulative frequency as then the median frequency is 50%. Figure 1 below is the cumulative frequency ogive for the length of bolts and you will see that the median is 50mm. So 50% of bolts are below 50mm in length and 50% above.

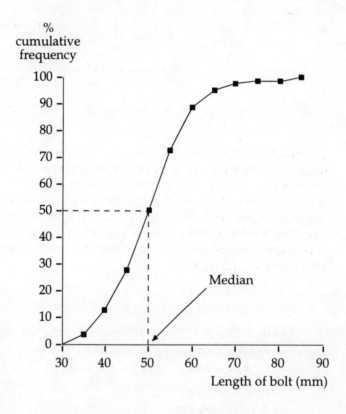

Figure 1

It is normal to talk about a *modal class* in a grouped frequency distribution although it is possible to estimate a single value. The grouped frequency table in Example 3 suggests that the intervals 45 to under 50mm and 50 to under 55mm have the highest frequency of 18. If these intervals had been separated, the distribution would have said to have been *bimodal*. Since they are together the modal class is 45 to 55mm. A single estimate of the modal value could be obtained using the geometric method illustrated in Figure 1 below. You should see that this modal value is approximately 50.5mm.

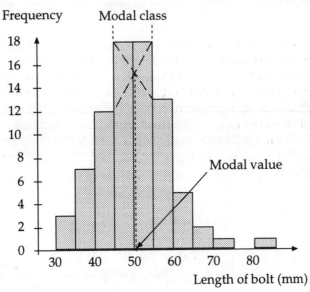

Figure 2

You might have noticed that all three averages are very similar. This is because the underlying distribution is approximately *symmetrical*. If the distribution was *right* skewed the mean would be displaced to the *right* of the mode and if the distribution was *left* skewed the mean would be displaced to the *left* of the mode. The median is between the two but closer to the mean. (Skewness was first discussed in Chapter 2, page 26). Earnings data is a good example of a distribution that is right skewed. This is because most people earn very little but a relatively few earn a great deal more, which distorts the mean value.

Activity 12

The grouped frequency table below refers to the weight of jars of coffee. What is the average weight of a jar according to this data?

Class Interval	Frequency
less than 96g	5
96 to under 98g	10
98 to under 99g	15
99 to under 100g	27
100 to under 102g	11
more than 102g	2

The problem with this table is the open classes. A mean needs a mid point for each interval, which this data clearly does not have. There is no satisfactory way of calculating the mean for grouped frequency tables with open classes although some people say you should use the width of the previous or next interval. So the mid point of the first interval would be 95g and 103g for the last interval. This approximation *may* be justified if the number of items in the open intervals are small relative to the closed intervals. I think that for open intervals the median is a far better average to use. The median only requires the upper value of each interval and it is not necessary for the ogive to be complete. This is illustrated in Figure 3 below where you will see that the median is about 99.2g.

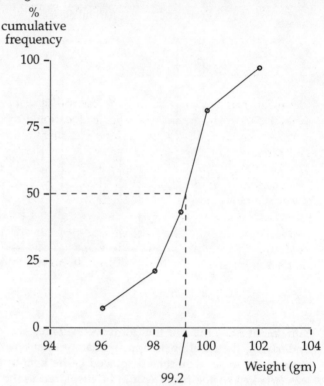

Figure 3

In the calculation of the mean each value was given an equal weighting. However, there are some circumstances where this is not correct. The next activity illustrates a typical example.

Activity 13

The pay rises given to 1000 employees during the year was as follows:

Employee	Pay rise	No. of employees
Manual	1%	700
Clerical	3%	200
Management	8%	100

The company maintains that the average pay rise was 4%. Is this correct?

The company has ignored the fact that the majority of the employees have received 3% or less. To get a better idea of the true average the percentages should be *weighted* by the number of employees in each category, as follows:

$$\frac{1 \times 700 + 3 \times 200 + 8 \times 100}{1000} = 2.1\%$$

This figure is much more representative of the true average pay rise.

3.3 Measures of spread

An average is not always sufficient in describing how a set of data is distributed. The sales data given in Example 1 is a typical example. This data has been reproduced below.

Mike: 3, 2, 1, 32, 2, 1, 1
Janet: 0, 1, 4, 12, 10, 7, 8, 6

The mean number of sales in both cases was 6 yet the individual figures are quite different. In addition to a measure of location a measure of *spread or dispersion* can also be provided. There are various measures of spread, the simplest is the range. The range is the difference between the smallest and largest and for Mike this is $32 - 1 = 31$ sales, while for Janet it is $12 - 0 = 12$. So there is a much larger spread in Mike's figures than in Janets'. Unfortunately the range is too easily influenced by extreme values and is not a particularly good measure. Another measure is the interquartile range (IQR). To calculate the IQR the data is divided into quarters. If Q1 is the lower quartile and Q3 is the upper quartile then IQR = Q3 – Q1 (Q2 is the median). This method avoids the extremes and so is more representative than the range. It is normally used with a group frequency table.

Activity 14

Calculate the IQR for the data given in Example 3.

The easiest method is to draw a cumulative frequency ogive and mark the 25% and 75% limits. This has been done in Figure 4 and you will see that the IQR is about $56 - 44 = 12$mm

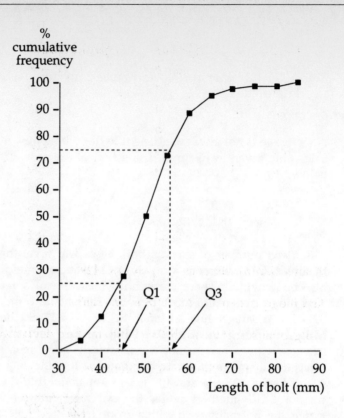

Figure 4

Unfortunately this is still not ideal because you are just looking at the middle half of the data and ignoring the rest. A better method is the standard deviation.

3.3.1 *The standard deviation*

A better measure of spread is to calculate the differences between each value and the mean as this will then use all the values. However, you now have as many values as you started with. You could find the average of all these differences, but since some differences will be positive and some negative you will end up with a mean of zero! You could ignore the negative sign but a better method (statistically) is to square the differences, as a negative value squared becomes a positive value. If you now average all these squared differences you will end up with an average squared difference. Both the range and IQR were in the same units as the original data so it would be good if this new measure was also in the same units. This can be arranged by taking the *square root* of the squared average. This procedure is shown below for Mike's sales data (remember the mean was 6).

Sales	Difference	Difference squared
x	$x - 6$	$(x - 6)^2$
3	-3	9
2	-4	16
1	-5	25
32	26	676
2	-4	16
1	-5	25
1	-5	25
Total		792

Mean squared difference $= \dfrac{792}{7} = 113.1429$

And the square root of 113.1429 is 10.6 sales

In algebraic terms the formula for the standard deviation is:

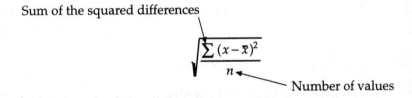

Sum of the squared differences

$$\sqrt{\frac{\sum (x - \bar{x})^2}{n}}$$

Number of values

Activity 15

Calculate the standard deviation for Janet's sales data.

You should have obtained a value of 3.9 sales and this demonstrates without doubt that Janet has a much smaller variation in her sales.

Activity 16

It has been discovered that a mistake has been made in Janet's sales data given in Example 1. Her daily sales are all 3 less than they should be. What should the mean and standard deviation really be?

You should have found the mean to be 9, which is simply 3 more than originally quoted. However, the standard deviation hasn't changed at 3.9. Why is this? This can be explained if you look at Figure 5 below. The original values have been shifted 3 units to the right. The spread of the new values has not changed so the standard deviation will be the same.

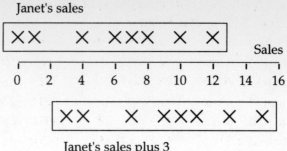

Janet's sales

Janet's sales plus 3

Figure 5

Activity 17

If Janet's sales should really be double the figures given in Example 1, what would the mean and standard deviation be in this case?

You should have found that both the mean and standard deviation has doubled. By doubling each value the spread has also doubled as you can see in Figure 6.

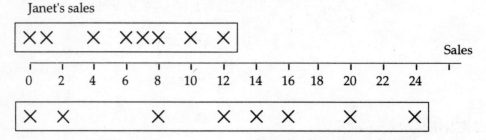

Janet's sales

Janet's sales times 2

Figure 6

3.3.2 *The standard deviation for a frequency distribution*

A slightly different formula is used for a frequency distribution to reflect the fact that frequencies are involved. The formula normally used is:

Sum of (f times x^2)   Sum of (f times x)

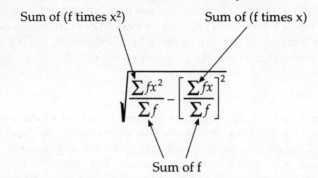

$$\sqrt{\frac{\sum fx^2}{\sum f} - \left[\frac{\sum fx}{\sum f}\right]^2}$$

Sum of f

Activity 18

Calculate the standard deviation of the data in Example 3.

The value of 'x' takes the same mid point value as in the calculation of the mean (Activity 9). The table becomes:

Interval	x	f	fx	x^2	fx^2
30 to under 35mm	32.5	3	97.5	1056.25	3168.75
35 to under 40mm	37.5	7	262.5	1406.25	9843.75
40 to under 45mm	42.5	12	510.0	1806.25	21675.0
45 to under 50mm	47.5	18	855.0	2256.25	40612.5
50 to under 55mm	52.5	18	945.0	2756.25	49612.5
55 to under 60mm	57.5	13	747.5	3306.25	42981.25
60 to under 65mm	62.5	5	312.5	3906.25	19531.25
65 to under 70mm	67.5	2	135.0	4556.25	9112.5
70 to under 75mm	72.5	1	72.5	5256.25	5256.25
75 to under 80mm	77.5	0	0	6006.25	0
80 to under 85mm	82.5	1	82.5	6806.25	6806.25
Total		80	4020		208600

The standard deviation is therefore:

$$\sqrt{\frac{208600}{80} - \left(\frac{4020}{80}\right)^2} = \sqrt{2607.5 - 2525.0625}$$

$$= \sqrt{82.4375}$$

$$= 9.08 \text{ mm}$$

3.4 Coefficient of variation

If two sets of data have similar means then it is easy to compare the variation by calculating their standard deviations. However, if the means are different then the comparisons of spread will not be so obvious.

Activity 19

A hospital is comparing the times patients are waiting for two types of operation. For bypass surgery the mean wait is 17 weeks with a standard deviation of 6 weeks, while for hip replacement the mean is 11 months with a standard deviation of 1 month. Which operation has the highest variability?

The problem here is not only that the means are quite different but the units are different (weeks in one case and months in the other). In order to compare the variability the coefficient of variation is calculated. This is defined as:

$$\frac{\text{Standard deviation}}{\text{mean}}$$

This is usually expressed as a percentage by multiplying by 100.

For bypass surgery the coefficient of variation is:

$$\frac{6}{17} \times 100 = 35.3\%$$

while for hip replacement it is:

$$\frac{1}{11} \times 100 = 9.1\%$$

Therefore relative to the mean the bypass surgery has a larger spread or variation.

3.5 Box and whisker plots

A very useful diagram that summarises information about the location and spread of a set of data is the box and whisker plot. The 'box' represents the middle 50% of the data and the extremities of the box are the quartiles Q1 and Q3. The median (Q2) is marked and will obviously be inside the box. Each 'whisker' represents 25% of the data and the extremities of the whiskers are the minimum and upper values of the data (or the class intervals).

Activity 20

Draw a box and whisker plot for the data given in Example 3.

The median (Q2) of this data is 50mm (see Activity 10) and the values of Q1 and Q3 are 44 and 56mm respectively (Activity 14). The box and whisker is shown below.

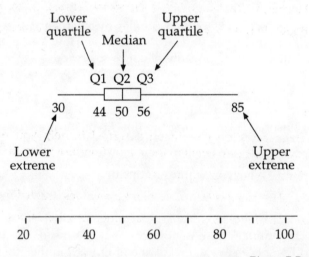

Figure 7 Box and whisker plot

Not only does this diagram give you an idea of the average and spread it also gives tells you about the shape of the distribution of the data. If the box is small compared to the whiskers this indicates a distribution that is bunched in the middle with long tails. A box shifted to one side or the other indicates skewness as does the position of the median within the box. In the case of the bolt lengths the right hand whisker is slightly longer than the left suggesting a slight right skewness to the distribution.

However, the median is exactly in the middle of the box so this skewness is very small. The box and whisker plot is particularly useful when you have two or more distributions to compare.

3.6 Summary

In this chapter you have seen the importance of calculating measures of location and spread for sets of data. The mean, median and mode each have their uses in describing the location of data. The mean is easier to calculate than the median but can be distorted by extreme values. The median is the middle value of a set of data that has been arranged in ascending order and is usually one of the data values. The easiest method of finding the median for a frequency distribution is to plot a cumulative frequency ogive. The mode is less useful that either the mean or the median but can be a good measure if you want to know the most common value or interval of a set of data. The mean, median and mode will be equal for a symmetrical distribution but for a right skewed distribution the mean and median will be greater than the mode and for a left skewed distribution they will be less than the mode. As well as an average it is useful to be able to give some indication of the spread or dispersion of a set of data. The range is the simplest measure but a better measure is the interquartile range. The IQR uses the middle 50% of the data and is therefore less influenced by extreme values. The standard deviation represents the average deviation from the mean and is the universally accepted measure of spread. If you want to compare the spread of two or more distributions it is useful to compare the coefficient of variation as this takes into account differences in the mean. Finally this chapter introduced you to a box and whisker plot, which is a very good way of summarising the information on location and spread of a frequency distribution.

3.7 Further reading

Morris, C, *Quantitative Approaches in Business Studies*, Pitman, 1993, Chapter 6

Harper, W, *Statistics, M & E Handbook Series*, Pitman, 1991, Chapter 10.

Booth, D.J, *A First Course in Statistics*, DP Publications, 1992, Chapter 4.

3.8 Exercises

Progress questions

These question have been designed to help you remember the key points in this chapter. The answers to these questions are given in Appendix 1, page 133.

Give the missing word in each case:

1. The mean is the .... of all the values divided by the number of values.

2. The median is the .... value once the values have been arranged in ascending order.

3. The mode is the value that occurs most ....

4. The .... is the simplest measure of spread.

5. The interquartile range represents the middle ....% of the data.

6. The standard deviation represents the mean .... from the mean.

7. The coefficient of variation is the ratio of the .... to the mean.

8. A box and whisker plot allows the .... of the distribution to be observed.

Answer TRUE or FALSE

9. The mean is usually one of the data values.

True ☐ False ☐

10. The mean is easy to calculate.

True ☐ False ☐

11. The median divides the data exactly in half.

True ☐ False ☐

12. The modal class is the middle of a distribution.

True ☐ False ☐

13 A symmetrical distribution always has a mean and median with the same value

True ☐ False ☐

14. To calculate the mean of grouped data it is necessary to 'sum the mid-interval values, multiply by the total of the frequencies and then divide by the total frequency'

True ☐ False ☐

Review questions

These questions have been designed to help you check your comprehension of the key points in this chapter. You may wish to look further than this chapter in order to answer them fully. You will find the reading list useful in this respect. You can check the essential elements of your answers by referring to the appropriate section.

15. Compare and contrast the essential differences of the 3 types of average. (Section 3.2)

16. What does the standard deviation tell you about a set of data? (Section 3.3.1)

17. What information does a box and whisker plot give you? (Section 3.5)

Multiple choice questions

The answers to these will be given in the Lecturers' Supplement.

The questions 18 to 25 refer to the series 3,1,4,2,3 represented by X

18. The value of $\sum X^2$ is:
   A   58
   B   582
   C   2704

19. The value of $(\sum X)^2$ is :
   A   2704
   B   582
   C   512

20. The MEAN of the series is :

    A 10.4

    B 10.0

    C 20.6

21. The MEDIAN of the series is :

    A 8

    B 10

    C 10.5

22. The RANGE of the series is :

    A 3

    B 5

    C 8

23. The STANDARD DEVIATION (to 1 decimal place) of the series is :

    A 28.7

    B 2.9

    C 0.3

24. The COEFFICIENT OF VARIATION (to 1 decimal place) is :

    A 27.6%

    B 362.4%

    C 0.3%

25. If the number 10 is added to each value of X, the STANDARD DEVIATION of the series is:

    A 28.7

    B 38.7

    C 2.9

    D 12.9

Practice questions

Answers to these questions will be given in the Lecturers' Supplement.

26. The weekly gross pay of 5 employees was as follows:

        £160.24, £183.56, £155.00, £274.50, £174.34

    a) Calculate the mean and median of the data. Which average may be more appropriate and why?

    b) Calculate the standard deviation of the data.

    c) Recalculate the mean and standard deviation if:

        i) each value is increased by £20

        ii) each value is increased by 5%

27. The weighting given to coursework and exam for a quantitative methods course at a university is 40% coursework and 60% exam. If a student gets 74% for the coursework and 56% in the exam, what would be her average mark for the unit?

28. The average lifetime for 12 light bulbs is 180.6 hours. Another light bulb gave a lifetime of 200 hours. What would the mean lifetime be if this result was included?

29. The sickness records of a company have been examined and the table below shows the number of days taken off work through sickness during the past year.

Days off work	Number of employees
Less than 2 days	45
2 to 5 days	89
6 to 9 days	40
10 to 13 days	25
14 to 21 days	5
22 to 29 days	2

a) What is the mean number of days off work?

b) What is the median number of days off work?

c) What is the modal number of days off work?

d) What is the interquartile range?

e) What is the standard deviation?

f) What is the coefficient of variation?

g) Draw a box and whisker plot and comment on the shape of the distribution.

30. Items are manufactured to the same nominal length on two different machines A and B. A number of items from each machine are measured and the results are as follows:

Class interval (mm)	Frequency Machine A	Machine B
20 to under 22	5	2
22 to under 24	12	5
24 to under 26	26	20
26 to under 28	11	25
28 to under 30	3	8
30 to under 32	0	2

a) Find the mean, median and modal values for the two machines.

b) Find the interquartile range and standard deviation for both machines.

c) Calculate the coefficient of variation for both machines.

d) Draw a box and whisker plot for both machines.

e) Use your results from (a) to (d) to comment on the lengths of items produced by both machines.

Assignment:

Answers to this assignment are included in the Lecturers' supplement.

A large bakery regularly takes samples of bread in order to ensure that its product meets quality specifications. Each loaf that is sampled is first weighed and weight records of 765 'standard' sliced loaves have accumulated over the last few months. The Quality Control Manager would like these records analysed and has aggregated the data into the frequency table shown below.

Weight range		Number of loaves in this range
780g to below 790g		34
790g	795g	80
795g	800g	111
800g	805g	162
805g	810g	161
810g	815g	120
815g	820g	70
820g	830g	27

Analyse these figures and write a report to the quality control manager. Your analysis should include graphs, diagrams and measures of location and spread of the data.

4 Probability and decision-making

4.1 Introduction

Most decisions have to be made when the outcome is not known with certainty. For example, should a new product be introduced if there is a chance that it will be a failure. or should an oil company drill for oil if there is a chance that the well will be dry? Before you are able to solve these and other decision problems you need to have a good understanding of the 'laws of chance'. This chapter contains all the basic rules and methods of probability and decision analysis that you will need to solve decision problems.

At the end of this chapter you should be able to:

☐ Calculate simple probabilities.

☐ Calculate probabilities of compound events using the rules of addition and multiplication.

☐ Use probability trees to solve problems.

☐ Calculate expected monetary values.

☐ Solve decision problems using decision trees.

4.2 Basic ideas

The value of a probability can be given either as a fraction, a decimal or as a percentage. An event with a probability of zero is termed impossible while an event with a probability of 1 or 100% is termed certain. Figure 1, below may help you picture the idea of the probability measure.

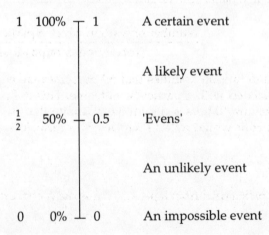

Figure 1

Probabilities can be obtained in a number of ways. The simplest is the *subjective* method where you estimate what you think the probability of a particular event will be. For example, a sales manager may estimate that the probability of high sales for a particular product is 60%. This figure may be based on market research or experience of a similar product but it is unlikely to involve any calculations.

Another method is the *empirical* approach. This method uses measurement to estimate probabilities. For example you may wish to decide the probability of a defective electrical component being produced by a particular process. If you test 100 components and find 5 defective then you would say that the probability of a defective component being produced is $\frac{5}{100}$ or 0.05.

That is probability $= \dfrac{\text{Number of times a particular event occured}}{\text{Total number of trials or 'experiments'}}$

The particular event here is finding a defective component and the 'experiment' is picking, testing and classifying a component as either good or defective.

Activity 1

Toss a coin 10 times and use the above formula to calculate the probability of a head.

Did you get a probability of 0.5? This, as you will see shortly is the 'correct' answer but 10 tosses is a very small number of experiments. If you tossed the coin a further 10 times you would quite likely get a different answer. This is the basis of *sampling error*, which we shall come back to in a later chapter (Chapter 6). You will also see that the sampling error in this case could be reduced by tossing the coin a larger number of times; that is the larger the number of tosses the nearer you will get to a probability of 0.5.

However, to obtain the theoretical probability of a head you would use a different method, called the a *priori* approach. This is similar to the empirical approach except that you can work out *in advance* how many times a particular event should occur. In the coin tossing activity you know that there is only one head so that the probability of a head is $\frac{1}{2}$ or 0.5.

If you picked a card from a pack, the probability of an ace is $\frac{4}{52}$ since there are 4 aces in a pack. The definition can be written as:

$$\frac{\text{Number of ways in which a particular event can occur}}{\text{Total number of possible outcomes}}$$

This definition assumes that all outcomes are equally likely; that is, there is no bias associated with a particular outcome. This definition would not apply to say a race involving 10 horses since the probability that any horse will win is unlikely to be 0.1. The odds would reflect such factors as form, jockey, trainer, etc.

Activity 2

You pick a card from a pack. What is the probability that it is a picture card?

To answer this question you would have listed the picture cards in a suit. These are Jack, Queen, King and Ace. Since there are 4 suits you should have decided that there will be $4 \times 4 = 16$ ways in which a particular outcome can occur. The probability of a picture card is therefore $\frac{16}{52} = 0.3077$.

4.3 The probability of compound events

It is frequently required to find the probability of two or more events happening at the same time. For example an aircraft has many of its controls duplicated so that if one fails the other one would still function. But what is the probability that both systems will fail? The way that probabilities are combined depend on whether the events are *independent* or whether they are *mutually exclusive.* Two (or more) events are said to be independent if the occurrence of one does not effect the occurrence of the other. The two aircraft systems will be independent if the failure of one system does not change the probability of failure of the other system. Two (or more) events are mutually exclusive if either event can occur but not both. One card drawn from a pack cannot be a Jack and an ace. However a Jack and a diamond are not mutually exclusive since the selected card could be both. When the set of all possible outcomes are known they are said to be *mutually exhaustive* and the sum of the probabilities of a set of outcomes that are mutually exclusive *and* mutually exhaustive must equal 1. For example, there are four suits in a pack of cards and the probability of selecting a card from either suit is $\frac{13}{52}$ or 0.25 . The sum of these probabilities is 1 since a card must come from one (and only one) of the suits. This idea will allow you to calculate a probability if the other or others are known. If say, the probability of a defective component is 5% then the probability that it is not defective is 95%.

Compound events can be more easily solved if a diagram is drawn. One useful diagram is the Venn diagram. A Venn diagram is made up of a square, the inside of which encloses all possible outcomes. The events of interest are represented by circles. The Venn diagram in Figure 2 represents two events A and B. Event A is being dealt a Jack, which has a probability of $\frac{4}{52}$ or 0.0769 while event B is being dealt an ace, which also has a probability of $\frac{4}{52}$.

The probability of being dealt either a Jack or an ace is:

$$P(\text{Jack or Ace}) = P(\text{Jack}) + P(\text{Ace})$$

$$= 0.0769 + 0.0769$$

$$= 0.1538$$

However if event B is being dealt a Diamond then the two events overlap as shown in Figure 3. If the two probabilities are now added the intersection of the two events (shown shaded) will have been added twice. This intersection, which represents the case of being dealt a Jack of Diamonds (with a probability of $\frac{1}{52}$ or 0.0192), must be subtracted from the sum of the two probabilities. That is

$$P(\text{Jack or Diamond}) = P(\text{Jack}) + P(\text{Diamond}) - P(\text{Jack of Diamonds})$$

$$= 0.0769 + 0.25 - 0.0192 = 0.3077$$

A = 'Jack'   B = 'Ace'   A = 'Jack'   B = 'Diamond'

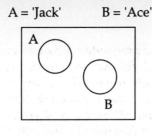

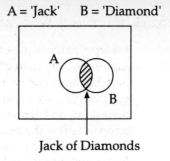

Jack of Diamonds

Figure 2   *Figure 3*

In general if P(A) means the probability of event A and P(B) the probability of event B then

$$P(A \text{ or } B) = P(A) + P(B) - P(A \text{ and } B)$$

This is known as the *addition* rule.

Note: If the two events are mutually exclusive as in the first example then there is no intersection and P(A and B) is zero.

Activity 3

The police regularly carry out spot checks on heavy goods vehicles. During one particular month the results are as follows:

	Overweight	Not overweight	Total
Driving time exceeded	15	25	40
Driving time not exceeded	20	40	60
Total	35	65	100

Assuming that these results are typical of all heavy goods vehicles on the road, what is the probability that if a vehicle was stopped at random it would either be overweight or the driver would have exceeded the allowed driving time?

The key to this question is the word 'or'. And since it is possible for both the vehicle to be overweight and the driver to have exceeded the permitted driving time, the events are not mutually exclusive. Using the addition law you should have obtained the following result:

$$P(\text{time exceeded}) = \frac{40}{100} \text{ or } 0.4 \quad P(\text{overweight}) = \frac{35}{100} \text{ or } 0.35$$

$$P(\text{time exceeded and overweight}) = \frac{15}{100} \text{ or } 0.15$$

So the P(time exceeded or overweight) $= 0.4 + 0.35 - 0.15$

$$= 0.6$$

That is there is a 60% chance that either the lorry would be overweight or the driver would have exceeded his driving time.

4.4 Conditional probability

If the probability of event B occurring is dependent on whether event A has occurred you would say that event B is conditional on event A and is written $P(B|A)$ which means probability of B, given A has occurred.

When events A and B are independent $P(B|A) = P(B)$. Sampling without replacement is a good example of conditional probability. If two students are to be chosen randomly from a group of 5 girls and 4 boys then the probability that the first person chosen is a girl is $\frac{5}{9}$ or 0.5556 and the probability it is a boy is 1 -0.5556 = 0.4444.

The probability that the second person is a girl depends on the outcome of the first choice.

First choice	Probability of second choice being a girl
boy	$\frac{5}{8}$ or 0.625
girl	$\frac{4}{8}$ or 0.5

In the first case the number of girls remains at 5 but in the second case there are only 4 girls to choose from. Note that in both cases the total number of students left is 8 since one has already been chosen.

If you want to know the probability of the first student being a girl and the second student being a girl you will need to use the *multiplication rule*. If the events are dependent as in this example, the rule is:

$$P(A \text{ and } B) = P(A) \times P(B|A)$$

So: $P(\text{girl and a girl}) = 0.5556 \times 0.5$
$$= 0.2778$$

If two (or more) events are independent the rule simplifies to:

$$P(A \text{ and } B) = P(A) \times P(B)$$

For example if an aircraft has a main and a back-up computer and the probability of failure of either computer is 1% then the probability of both failing is .01 × .01 = .0001 or .01%.

Activity 4

A light bulb manufacturer produces bulbs in batches of 50 and it is known that 5 of each batch will be defective. If two bulbs are selected without replacement from a batch, what is the probability that both will be defective?

The probability that the first bulb is defective is $\frac{5}{50}$ = 0.1 but the probability that the second is defective is $\frac{4}{49}$ = 0.0816 since the total number of bulbs has been reduced by one and there must be one less defective bulb. The probability that both bulbs are defective is therefore:

$$0.1 \times 0.0816 = 0.00816$$

This probability is very small so if you did in fact get two defective bulbs you should be suspicious concerning the claimed defective rate. (This idea forms the basis of some quality control schemes).

4.5 Tree diagrams

A very useful diagram to use when solving compound events, particularly when conditional probability is involved, is the tree diagram. This diagram represents different outcomes of an experiment by means of branches. For example, in the student example the two 'experiments' of choosing an individual can be represented by the tree diagram in Figure 4. The first experiment is represented by a small circle or node and the two possible outcomes are represented by branches radiating out from the node. The event and probability are written alongside the branch. The second experiment is again represented by a node and you will notice that this node appears twice, once for each outcome of the first experiment. Branches again radiate out from each node but notice that the probability is different depending on what happened in the first experiment.

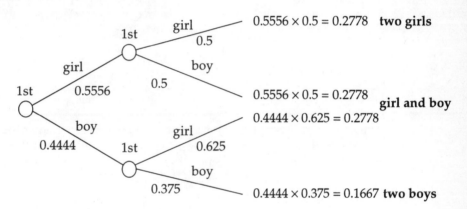

Figure 4

You will see that the compound events have been written at the end of each route in Figure 4. If you add up these probabilities you will see that they sum to 1. This is because the routes are mutually exclusive and *mutually exhaustive*. They are mutually exclusive because one and only one of the routes can be followed and they are mutually exhaustive because all possible routes have been shown. From this diagram various probabilities could be evaluated using the law of addition. For example the probability of getting two students of the same sex is 0.2778 + 0.1667 = 0.4445.

It is unlikely that you would use a tree diagram to solve a simple problem like this, but consider the following problem.

The demand for gas is dependent on the weather and much research has been undertaken to accurately forecast the demand. This is important since it is quite difficult (and expensive) to increase the supply at short notice. If, on any particular day, the air temperature is below normal, the probability that the demand will be high is 0.6. However, at normal temperatures the probability of a high demand occurring is only 0.2 and if the temperature is above normal the probability of a high demand drops to 0.05. What is the probability of a high demand occurring if over a period of time the temperature is below normal 20% of occasions and above normal 30% of occasions?

The tree diagram is shown in Figure 5, below. Since the demand *depends* on temperature the first node refers to temperature and there are three branches; below, normal and above normal.

The probability of the temperature being normal is $1 - (0.2 + 0.3) = 0.5$.

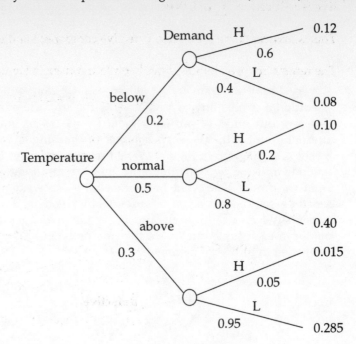

Figure 5

The compound probability for each route has been written at the end of the route, so that the probability of there being a high demand given that the temperature is below normal is $0.2 \times 0.6 = 0.12$. Since there are three routes where the demand could be high, the law of addition is used and the probability is

$$0.12 + 0.10 + 0.015 = 0.235$$

Activity 5

A company purchases electronic components in batches of 100 and the supplier guarantees that there will be no more than 5 defective components in each batch. Before acceptance of a particular batch the company has a policy of selecting without replacement two components for testing. If both components are satisfactory the batch is accepted and if both are defective the batch is rejected. However, if only one is defective another component is selected and if this is satisfactory the batch is accepted while if it is defective the batch is rejected. If the probability that a component is defective is 5%, what is the probability that the batch will be accepted?

You could answer this question without a tree diagram but it is strongly recommended that diagrams are used whenever possible. The diagram is shown in Figure 6 below where it will be seen that each node has two outcomes; either o.k or defective. At the start of the process the probability that the first selection will give a defective component is $\frac{5}{100}$ or 0.05 and the probability that it will be o.k is 0.95.

If the first component was defective then the probability that the second is also defective is reduced to $\frac{4}{99}$ or 0.04040.

This is because there is one less defective component and one less component in total.

The remaining probabilities have been found using a similar reasoning.

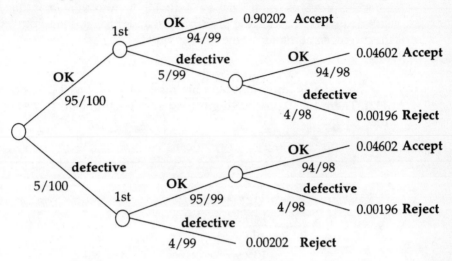

Figure 6

The compound probabilities have been written at the end of each route together with the decision; that is, accept or reject. There are three routes where the decision is to accept and the addition law can be used to give the probability that the batch will be accepted. That is:

$$0.90202 + 0.04602 + 0.0462 = 0.99406$$

The probability that the batch will be rejected is $1 - 0.99406 = 0.00594$. This can be confirmed by adding the probabilities separately.

As in Activity 4, it is unlikely that a batch would be rejected. However if it was you would have grounds to question the supplier about the true number of defective items in a batch. This type of problem comes under the category of quality control, which is discussed in more detail in *'Quantitative Approaches to Decision making'*, by the same author.

4.6 Permutations and combinations

Problems frequently exist where selections are made from groups of items. In these cases it is useful to be able to calculate the number of selections that are possible. The method used depends on whether the order of the selection is important or not. If it is you should use *permutations*. The number of permutations, where r items are to be selected from a group of size n is given by the formula:

$$^{n}P_{r} = \frac{n!}{(n-r)!}$$

where $n!$ is read as *'factorial n'* and means $(n-1)\times(n-2)\times(n-3)\times....$

For example, $5! = 5 \times 4 \times 3 \times 2 \times 1 = 120$ (Note: $1! = 1$ and by definition $0! = 1$). If you have a scientific calculator you should find that np_r can be obtained directly.

Activity 6

Bank cheque cards usually have a 4 digit 'pin' number so that they can be used in a cash dispenser. What is the probability that a thief, finding your card, could hit on the correct combination at the first attempt?

The order is important here because, for example, 1234 is a different number to 4321. There are 10 possible digits (0 to 9) so the number of ways of selecting 4 from 10 is:

$$^nP_r = {}^{10}P_4$$

$$= \frac{10!}{(10-4)!}$$

$$= \frac{10!}{6!}$$

$$= \frac{10 \times 9 \times 8 \times 7 \times 6 \times 5 \times 4 \times 3 \times 2 \times 1}{6 \times 5 \times 4 \times 3 \times 2 \times 1}$$

$$= 5040$$

So there is only a 1 in 5040 chance of the thief finding the correct permutation. As a probability this is:

$$\frac{1}{5040} = 0.000198$$

Where the order is not important you would use *combinations*. The formula for this is as follows:

$$^nC_r = \frac{n!}{r!(n-r)!}$$

Again most scientific calculators should contain this function.

Activity 7

What is the probability of getting 4 heads from 10 tosses of a coin?

Order here is not important since 4 heads followed by 6 tails is no different to 6 tails followed by 4 heads. The combination formula will therefore give you the number of ways of obtaining 4 heads from 10 tosses of a coin. That is:

$$^nC_r = {}^{10}C_4$$

$$= \frac{10!}{4!(10-4)!}$$

$$= \frac{10 \times 9 \times 8 \times 7 \times 6 \times 5 \times 4 \times 3 \times 2 \times 1}{4 \times 3 \times 2 \times 1 \times (6 \times 5 \times 4 \times 3 \times 2 \times 1)}$$

$$= 210$$

Since the probability of a head is 0.5 and each toss of the coin is independent, the probability of getting any combination of heads and tails must be $(0.5)^{10} = 0.0009765$. If you now try and picture the problem as a tree diagram you should realise that this is simply the compound probability of one route of the tree. Since 210 routes contain 4 heads, the probability of getting 4 heads in 10 tosses is:

$$210 \times 0.0009765 = 0.2051$$

4.7 Expected value

If you toss a coin 100 times, you would expect 50 heads and 50 tails. That is, the expected number of heads is $.5 \times 100 = 50$. In general it is a long-run average, which means it is the value you would get if you repeated the experiment long enough. It is calculated by multiplying a value of a particular variable by the probability of its occurrence and repeating this for all possible values. In symbols this can be represented as:

$$\text{Expected value} = \Sigma\, px$$

where Σ means the 'sum of'.

Activity 8

Over a long period of time a salesperson recorded the number of sales she achieves per day. From an analysis of her records it was found that she made no sales 20% of the time, one sale 50% of the time and 2 sales 30% of the time. What is her expected number of sales?

The 'x' in this case takes on values of 0, 1, and 2 and:

$$\text{expected value} = 0.2 \times 0 + 0.5 \times 1 + 0.3 \times 2$$

$$= 0 + 0.5 + 0.6$$

$$= 1.1 \text{ sales}$$

This is just like working out the mean value of a group of numbers, where the probabilities are the frequencies or 'weights'. And just like the mean, the expected value will not necessarily be a whole number.

Expected values are frequently used to calculate expected monetary values, or EMV. This is illustrated in the next activity.

Activity 9

An investor buys £1000 of shares with the object of making a capital gain after 1 year. She believes that there is a 5% chance that the shares will double in value, a 25% chance that they will be worth £1500, a 30% chance that they will only be worth £500 and a 40% chance that they will not change in value. What is the expected monetary value of this investment, ignoring dealing costs?

The EMV is found in a similar manner to the expected number of sales in Activity 1, that is:

$$\text{EMV} = 0.05 \times 2000 + 0.25 \times 1500 + 0.3 \times 500 + 0.40 \times 1000$$

$$= 100 + 375 + 150 + 400$$

$$= £1025$$

So the EMV is £1025, an expected profit of £25

4.8 Decision trees

Decision trees are similar to probability trees except that as well as probabilistic (or chance) branches there are also decision branches. Decision branches allow the decision maker to compare alternative options, while the chance branches handle the probabilistic nature of an outcome. The skeleton of a single stage decision tree is shown in Figure 7, below.

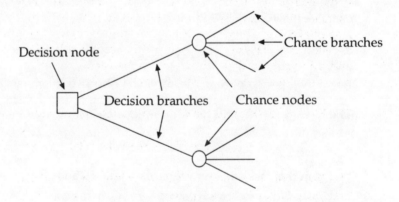

Figure 7

The square node represent the point where the decision is made, while the round nodes represent the point at which chance takes over. The decision tree is drawn from left to right but to evaluate the tree you work from right to left. This is called the 'roll-back' method. You first evaluate the EMV at each chance node and then at the decision node you select the 'best' EMV (don't forget, 'best' can be lowest cost as well as largest profit).

Example 1

A car accessory company, Marla Plc have developed a new car immobiliser and have to decide whether to market the product nationwide, to sell by mail order or to sell the patent to a large chain of motor accessory shops. The cost of distributing nationwide is very high but the potential profits could also be large. There is less risk with selling by mail order but the potential profits would also be less. The safe option is to sell the patent but in this case the chance of making large profits would be lost. How does Marla make their decision given that they have limited knowledge of the likely demand for the product? The estimated profits for each decision depends on the state of the market, which has been defined as high, medium and low. The probability that the state of the market will be either high, medium or low has been estimated as 0.25, 0.3, and 0.45 respectively. The expected profits (in £000's) is given in the table below.

Decision	State of the market		
	High (P=0.25)	Medium (P=0.3)	Low (P=0.45)
Nationwide	95	52	(26)
Mail order	48	24	19
Sell patent	25	25	25

Note: (26) means a loss of £26,000

Activity 10

What decision should the company make in order to maximise their EMV?

If the company distributed the product nationwide they would have a 0.25 or 25% chance of making £95,000 profit. However, there is also a 45% probability of making a loss of £26,000. The decision that maximises their EMV can be found by means of a decision tree. The decision tree for this problem has been drawn in Figure 8, below and you will see that the outcomes for each decision and state of the market have been written at the end of each probabilistic branch.

The EMV (in £000's) for the decision branch 'nationwide' is calculated as follows:

$$95 \times 0.25 + 52 \times 0.3 + (-26) \times 0.45 = £27.65$$

The EMV for the remaining two decisions are calculated similarly and is £27.75 for mail order and £25 for sell patent.

The three EMV's are now compared. The decision that gives the largest EMV is sell by mail order, although distributing nationwide is a close second.

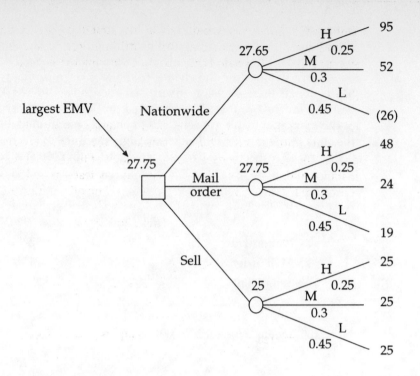

Figure 8

This was an example of a *single* stage decision problem. Decision trees are normally used where multi-stage decisions are involved and the following example illustrates a typical problem.

Example 2

The Delma oil company has obtained government approval to drill for oil in the Bristol Channel. This area is known to contain oil deposits and industry sources believe that there is a 50% chance oil will be found in a commercial viable quantity. The cost of the drilling programme is believed to be £30m. but this could be more than offset by the potential revenue, which is put at £100m at today's prices.

The company could carry out test drillings at different sites, which would only cost £5m. From historical data tests are likely to indicate a viable field 65% of the time. However these tests are not completely reliable and the probability that they are correct is only 0.7. That is, if the tests are positive there is a 70% chance that a viable quantity of oil will be found and if negative there is only a 30% (100 – 70) chance that oil will be found in a viable quantity.

The company could sell its rights to drill in the area but the revenue obtained will depend on the outcome of the tests (if carried out) and are as follows:

Tests indicate oil	£35m
Tests don't indicate oil	£3m
No tests carried out	£10m

Activity 11

What decisions should the company make given this information.

This problem involves two decisions. The first decision is whether to test drill and the second decision is whether to start its drilling programme. In order to solve this decision problem you would carry out the following three steps:

Step 1

Draw the decision tree. This is shown in Figure 9. You will see that the decision nodes have been numbered 1, 2, and 3 while the chance nodes have been labelled as a, b, c and d. The values at the end of each branch of the tree represent the net outcome. For instance, if drilling is carried out without any tests and oil is found, the net outcome is a profit of £100m – £30m = £70m, whereas if no oil is found a loss of £30m is made.

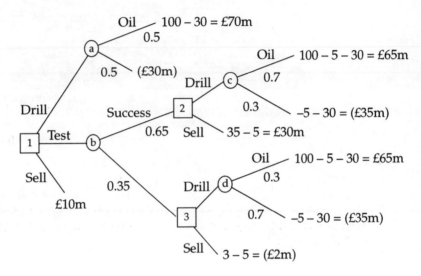

Figure 9

Step 2

Working from the right, the EMV at the chance nodes a, c and d are calculated as follows:

Node	EMV
a	$0.5 \times 70 + 0.5 \times (-30) = £20m$
c	$0.7 \times 65 + 0.3 \times (-35) = £35m$
d	$0.3 \times 65 + 0.7 \times (-35) = -£5m$

(The EMV at b cannot be calculated until step 3.)

Step 3

The roll-back technique is now employed. At decision node 2, the decision is to either drill or sell. Sell will give you £30m, whereas drilling will give you £35m. The option that gives the largest EMV is to drill and so this is the option that would be taken. The value 35 is put above node 2 and the sell option is crossed out. If you repeat this for node 3 you should find that the best option here is to sell. The EMV at chance node b can now be calculated and you should find that this is £22.05m ($0.65 \times 35 + 0.35 \times (-2)$). You can now go to decision node 1 and compare the three decisions. You should find the following:

Drill: £20m

Test: £22.05m

Sell: £10m

The best decision is to test first. If the test gives successful results, only then should drilling start; Otherwise the rights should be sold for £3m. You will see this analysis summarised in Figure 10, below.

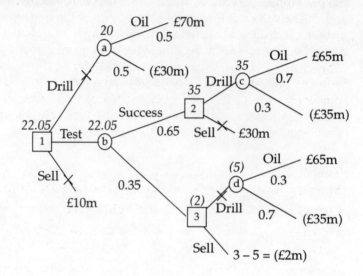

Figure 10

4.9 Sensitivity analysis

The major difficulty with decision analysis is estimating the probabilities and the expected returns. In many cases the probabilities are simply best guesses. In any decision analysis, the sensitivity of the recommended decision to changes in any of the estimated values should be investigated. This is particularly true for cases where the EMV values for two or more decisions are similar as in Example 2.

Activity 12

How much can the probability of a successful test in the Delma Oil company problem (Example 2) be allowed to vary before the decision changes from 'test first' to 'drill without test'?

To answer this question you could try different values of the probability but the easiest method is to call the probability 'p' and the EMV at node b then becomes:

$$35 \times p + (-2) \times (1 - p) \quad = 35p - 2 + 2p$$

$$= 37p - 2$$

The decision will change when the value of this expression is less than £20m.

That is:

$$37p - 2 \quad < 20$$

i.e $\qquad 37p \quad < 22$

therefore $\qquad p \quad < 0.595$

So the probability only has to fall from 0.65 to below 0.6 before the decision changes.

4.10 Summary

This chapter has introduced you to some of the basic rules of probability and shown you one important area of application. Probability can be used to calculate expected monetary values, which are used in solving decision problems. Decision trees are one method of solving decision problems and these are commonly used when one decision leads to others.

4.11 Further reading

Morris, C, *Quantitative Approaches in Business Studies*, Pitman, 1993, Chapter 7

Lucy, T, *Quantitative Techniques*, DP Publications, 1992, Chapter 2.

Oakshott, L, *Quantitative Approaches to Decision Making*, DP Publications, 1993, Units 1 and 5.

Goodwin and Wright, *Decision Analysis for Management Judgment*, Wiley, 1991, Chapter 5.

4.12 Exercises

Progress questions

These question have been designed to help you remember the key points in this chapter. The answers to these questions are given in Appendix 1, page 133.

Give the missing word in each case.

1. Probability is measured on a scale from 0 to ....

2 Probabilities that are obtained by measurement are called .... probabilities.

3. Probabilities that are obtained by guesses are called .... probabilities.

4. The sum of the probabilities of a series of mutually exclusive and mutually exhaustive events is ....

5. The .... law is used when you want to find the probability of event A occurring or event B.

6. The .... law is applicable when you want to find the probability that both events A and event B will occur.

7. EMV stands for .... monetary value.

8. Decision .... are a diagrammatic way of solving decision problems.

Answer TRUE or FALSE

9. Probability cannot exceed 1 or 100%

True ☐ False ☐

10. If you got 9 consecutive heads in 9 tosses of a coin then the next toss will almost certainly be a tail.

True ☐ False ☐

11. Two tosses of the same coin is an example of independent events.

True ☐ False ☐

12. The correct name for a combination lock is a permutation lock.

True ☐ False ☐

13. Expected value is a long run average

True ☐ False ☐

14. In a decision tree decision nodes are represented by circles.

True ☐ False ☐

Review questions

These questions have been designed to help you check your comprehension of the key points in this chapter. You may wish to look further than this chapter in order to answer them fully. You will find the reading list useful in this respect. You can check the essential elements of your answers by referring to the appropriate section.

15. Compare and contrast the different methods of obtaining probabilities. (Section 4.2)

16. Under what circumstances would the addition law of probability be used? (Section 4.3)

17. Under what circumstances would the multiplication law of probability be used? (Section 4.3)

18. What are the essential differences between permutations and combinations? (Section 4.6)

19. What are the essential features of a decision tree and how does it differ from a probability tree? (Sections 4.5 and 4.8)

Multiple choice questions

The answers to these will be given in the Lecturers' Supplement.

20. P(B | A) means:
    A   The probability of B divided by the probability of A
    B   The probability of B given that A has occurred
    C   The probability of A given that B has occurred
    D   The probability of A times B

21. If P(A) = P(A | B), the events A and B are
    A   Mutually exclusive
    B   Exhaustive
    C   Statistically independent

22. If three coins are tossed, the probability of exactly one head occurring is:

    A $\frac{3}{8}$

    B $\frac{2}{3}$

    C $\frac{1}{8}$

    D $\frac{1}{4}$

23. If two events, A and B, are statistically independent, the occurrence of A implies that the probability of B occurring will be:

    A 0

    B unchanged

    C 1

    D unknown

24. If a fair coin is tossed 9 times and a head is obtained on each toss, the probability that the next toss of the coin will produce a tail is:

    A 0

    B 0.5

    C 1.0

    D less than 0.5

    E more than 0.5

Practice questions

Answers to these questions will be given in the Lecturers' Supplement.

25. A bag contains 5 red discs, 3 yellow discs, and 2 green discs.

    a) A disc is picked from the bag. What is the probability that the disc will be:

        i) red   ii) yellow   iii) not yellow

    b) Two discs are picked from the bag with replacement. What is the probability that the discs will be:

        i) both red   ii) 1 red and 1 yellow

    c) Repeat part (b) if the discs are picked without replacement.

26. What is the probability that if you pick a card from a pack it will be:

    a) an ace

    b) a red card

    c) an ace or a red card

27. A box contains 50 light bulbs of which 4 are defective. You purchase two bulbs from this box. what is the probability that both will be defective?

28. The probability that a double glazing salesperson will make a sale on a particular day is 0.05. What is the probability that over a three day period the salesperson will make:

    a) 3 sales

    b) exactly 1 sale

    c) at least 1 sale

29. A mail order firm knows that it will receive a 20% response rate to any literature it circulates. In a new geographic location eight circulars are mailed as a market test. Assuming that the response rate is still applicable to this new location, calculate the probability of the following events:

i) All 8 people respond

ii) No one responds

iii) Exactly 2 people respond (Hint: first find the number of ways of choosing 2 from 8)

30 How might you try to assess the following probabilities:

a) the probability that the FT index will rise in value tomorrow.

b) the probability that a jar of coffee filled by an automatic process, will weigh less than the stated weight;

c) the probability that you might win the top prize in the national lottery

d) the probability that the ageing process will eventually be reversed.

31. A company intends to market a new product and it estimates that there is a 20% chance that it will be first in the market and this will give them £2m revenue in the first year. However, if they are not first in the market the expected revenue will only be £0.5m. What is the EMV?

32. Please refer to the diagram below for this question and note that the objective is to maximise EMV.

i) What is the value of X

ii) What is the EMV at probabilistic node B

iii) What is the EMV at probabilistic node C

iv) What should the decision be at decision node A (Decision 1 or Decision 2).

v) What should the value of X be in order that you will be indifferent to choosing between decision 1 and 2.

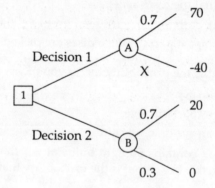

Assignment

Answers to this assignment are given in the Lecturers' Supplement.

Chix laboratory have recently come up with a method of producing joints of 'chicken' from non-animal products. The process is quite revolutionary and the taste and texture of the 'meat' is believed to be indistinguishable from the real thing. The product should also have an advantage in terms of price and shelf life (the product need not be stored in a refrigerator and will stay in good condition for up to two weeks).

However, the cost of setting up production is very high at £1m and it is not at all certain that consumers will accept the product. The marketing department have assessed the risk and believe that there is only a 30% chance that consumers will approve of the product. If consumers do approve then sales are estimated to be around £2.5m p.a, but if the reaction is negative then sales will amount to no more than £0.7m p.a (the catering market is virtually guaranteed to want the product).

The risk could be reduced by carrying out a survey to gauge public reaction to the product. From past experience this kind of survey produces accurate results 85% of the time. (That is, if the survey indicates a favourable response, the probability that a favourable response occurs is 0.85 and similarly, if the survey suggests a negative response, the probability that a negative response occurs is 0.85). The cost of this survey will be £100,000.

The product manager assigned to this new product line is Graham Green and he has requested your help in deciding whether to commission a survey or to proceed immediately with full production. You explain that the decision is perhaps more complicated than he thinks and the following options are available to him:

1. Proceed with full production

2. Commission a survey. Whatever the results of the survey there are two further options, that is proceed with full production or abandon the project.

3. Abandon the project.

Following discussions with the marketing department, you decide that carrying out the marketing survey before going into full production will not effect the expected sales revenue. You have also assumed that the probability that the survey will indicate a favourable response is 0.3.

a) Draw a decision tree for the problem and decide what the correct decisions should be.

b) Investigate the sensitivity of your answer changes to the probability of a favourable response.

5 *The normal distribution*

5.1 Introduction

This chapter examines a very important probability distribution called the normal distribution. This distribution has applications in almost all aspects of daily life, such as the deciding whether the weight of a loaf of bread is outside acceptable limits or whether a child's height or weight is abnormal in some way.

To complete this chapter successfully you should have already worked through Chapter 2 (Displaying data), Chapter 3 (Summarising data) and Chapter 4 (Probability and decision making).

On completing this chapter you should:

❏ Understand the difference between a continuous and discrete probability distribution.

❏ Understand how the shape of the normal distribution is affected by the mean and standard deviation of the data.

❏ Be able to use the normal distribution table.

5.2 Discrete and continuous probability distributions

The differences between discrete and continuous data were discussed in Chapter 2 (page 13) but essentially discrete data is obtained by *counting* whereas continuous data is obtained by *measurement*. So counting the number of loaves of bread baked over a period of time would give you data that only contained whole numbers (assuming that the bread is only sold as complete loaves), while recording the weight of each loaf of bread baked would give you data that could take on any value.

Example

Data on the number and weight of a 'standard' loaf of bread was collected over a period of time and aggregated into two frequency tables shown below:

Number of loaves baked		Weight of each loaf		
Number	Frequency	Weight range		Frequency
20	25	770g to below 775g		3
21	32	775g	780g	17
22	35	780g	785g	44
23	30	785g	790g	100
24	30	790g	795g	141
25	47	795g	800g	192
26	38	800g	805g	191
27	25	805g	810g	150
		810g	815g	90
		815g	820g	42
		820g	825g	14
		825g	830g	9

In order to compare the two data sets in more detail diagrams could be used. A bar chart would be appropriate for the number of loaves baked while a *histogram* is necessary for the weight data (see Chapter 2). These diagrams are shown below.

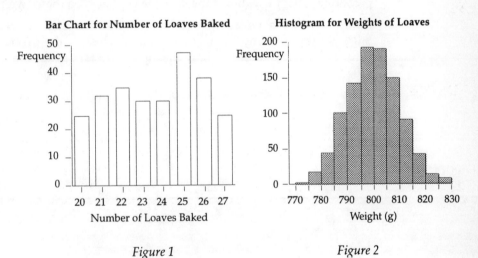

Figure 1   *Figure 2*

5.3 Properties of the normal distribution

In Chapter 2 you saw how to group data into a frequency table and then display this information as a histogram and as a frequency polygon. The frequency polygon gave you the underlying distribution of the data, that is, it showed you how the data was *distributed* across the range of possible values. This kind of distribution is called an *empirical* distribution because it is obtained by measurement or observation. There are also distributions that can be derived mathematically. The most important of these is the *normal* distribution.

Many observations that are obtained from measurements follow the normal distribution. For example the heights of people and the weights of loaves of bread are approximately normally distributed. The normal distribution is completely symmetrical or bell shaped. The mean, mode, and median of this distribution all lie at the centre of the bell as you can see in Figure 3, below.

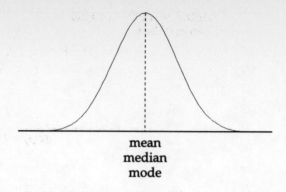

mean
median
mode

Figure 3

The normal curve has the following properties:

a) The curve is symmetrical about the mean.

b) The total area under the curve is equal to 1 or 100%. This means that probability can be equated to area.

c) The horizontal axis represents a continuous variable such as weight.

d) The area under the curve between two points on the horizontal axis represents the probability that the value of the variable lies between these two points.

e) As the distance between two points gets less, the area between the two points must get less. Taking this to its logical conclusion, the probability of a specific value is zero. It is therefore only meaningful to talk about ranges, such as 800g to 810g.

f) The position and shape of the curve depends on the mean and standard deviation of the distribution. As the standard deviation gets larger, the curve will get flatter and extend further on either side of the mean.

Activity 1

The average weight of a 'standard' loaf of bread is 800g and the weights are normally distributed. If a loaf is selected at random, what is the probability that it will weigh less than 800g?

Property (a) above says that the normal curve is symmetrical about the mean, so that 50% of the loaves will be below the mean weight of 800g and 50% will be above. Hence the probability will be 0.5 or 50%.

Activity 2

What proportion of loaves weigh more than 815g?

This problem has been illustrated diagrammatically in Figure 4, where the area representing all loaves with a weight exceeding 815g has been shaded.

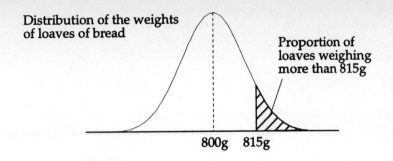

Distribution of the weights of loaves of bread

Proportion of loaves weighing more than 815g

800g 815g

Figure 4

This shaded area is clearly a small proportion of the total area but it would be difficult to estimate the actual figure from the diagram alone. Tables are used to obtain this area but before you can do this, you need to understand the properties of the *standard normal distribution*.

5.4 The standard normal distribution

The standard normal distribution has a mean of zero and a standard deviation of 1. This is illustrated in Figure 5, below. The figures along the horizontal axis are number of standard deviations and are called the Z values. You will see from the diagram that the majority of the distribution is covered within 3 standard deviations either side of the mean.

The standard normal distribution

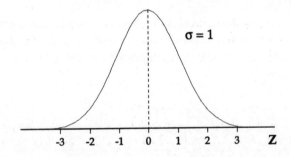

$\sigma = 1$

-3 -2 -1 0 1 2 3 **Z**

Figure 5

To demonstrate the use of the normal table you should now refer to the table provided in Appendix 2, page 135. The table provided in this book gives you the area in the *right hand tail* of the distribution but other tables may give the area in a different way. (Once you have used one table you should find it a simple matter to use a different type).

The first column gives the Z value to one decimal place and the first row gives the second place of decimals. For example, for a Z value of 0.55, you would look down the first column until you found 0.5 and then across until you were directly under .05. The area is 0.2912, or 29.12%. This is the area in the tail for Z being greater than 0.55. Since the distribution is symmetrical the area being less than $Z = -0.55$ is also 29.12%. You will see these areas shaded in Figure 6 below.

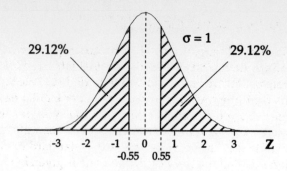

Figure 6

What is the area between a Z value of 1 and -1

The area of the curve for Z greater than 1 is 0.1587 or 15.87% To find the area from the mean to any Z value you need to use the fact that half the distribution has an area of 0.5. So to find the area from the mean to Z = 1 you would subtract this from 0.5. That is 0.5 – 0.1587 = 0.3413. since the distribution is symmetrical, the area from 0.0 to -1.0 is also 0.3413. The area from -1 to +1 is therefore 0.6826. In other words, 68.26% of the normal curve is covered by ± 1 standard deviations. This area can be seen in Figure 7 below.

If you repeat this for Z = 2 and Z = 3 you should find that just over 95% (95.44%) of the normal distribution is covered by ± 2 standard deviations and almost 100% (99.73%) is covered by ± 3 standard deviations.

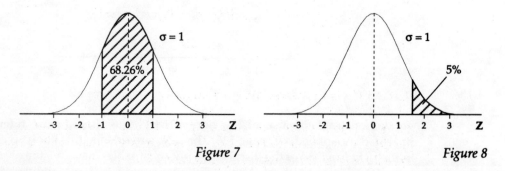

Figure 7   *Figure 8*

What is the value of Z if the area of the upper tail is 5%?

This problem is illustrated in Figure 8 above. To solve this problem the normal table is used in reverse. That is, the table is inspected to find the area of 0.05. This figure does not exist but you should find that a Z value of 1.64 gives an area of 0.0505 while a Z value of 1.65 gives an area of 0.0495. The most accurate value of Z would be the average of these two values, which is 1.645.

5.5 Standardising normal distributions

Unfortunately most normal distribution problems do not have a mean of zero or a standard deviation of 1 so the normal table cannot be used directly to solve general problems. However, all you have to do is to calculate the number of standard deviations from the mean, and this can be done quiet easily as follows. Subtract the mean value (μ) from the particular value that you are interested in and then divide this value by the standard deviation (s). For example, if the mean is 5 and the standard deviation is 2, then a value of 9 is two standard deviations from the mean. This calculation is called the Z *transformation* and is given by:

$$Z = \frac{x - \mu}{\sigma}$$

If x is less than μ the value of Z will be negative. This negative value simply indicates that x is to the left of the mean. Since the distribution is symmetrical about the mean you can ignore the sign when using the table.

Activity 5

A batch of loaves are baked. The weight of the loaves are normally distributed with a mean of 800g and a standard deviation of 10g. What proportion of loaves will weigh more than 815g?

This is the same problem that you met in Activity 2 (see Figure 4, page 77) but you now should be able to solve this using the normal table. However you first have to transform the problem using the Z formula. You should first note that:

$$\mu = 800g, \sigma = 10g \text{ and } x = 815g.$$

$$z = \frac{815 - 800}{10} = 1.5$$

That is, 815g is 1.5 standard deviations away from the mean.

It is now a simple matter of looking up Z = 1.5 in the normal table. If you do this you should get an area of 0.0668 or 6.68%, which means that 6.68% of all loaves weigh more than 815g. This is represented in Figure 9 below.

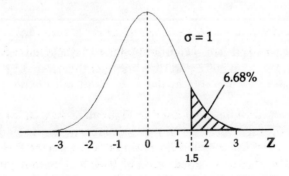

Figure 9

The problem can become slightly more difficult as illustrated in the next activity.

Activity 6

A loaf is chosen at random. What is the probability that the weight will lie between 810g and 812g?

To find the probability it is necessary to find the area shown shaded in Figure 10 below. This area cannot be found directly but it can be found by *subtracting* the area greater than 812 from the area greater than 810. To do this it is necessary to calculate two Z values as follows:

$$\frac{810-800}{10}=1.0 \quad and \quad \frac{812-800}{10}=1.2$$

The areas from the normal table are 0.1587 and 0.1157 and the required area is:

$$0.1587 - 0.1151 = 0.0436$$

The probability that the weight will be between 810g and 812g is therefore 0.0436 or 4.36%. Alternatively you could say that 4.36% of all loaves weigh between 810g and 812g.

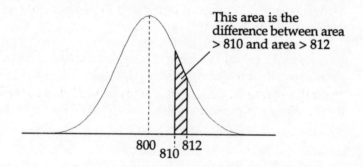

Figure 10

Activity 7

What proportion of loaves weigh between 790g and 805.5g

To solve this problem you should note that the required area is the *sum* of the two areas A and B (see Figure 11 below). To calculate area A it is necessary to find the area greater than 805.5 and then subtract this from 0.5 (Don't forget the tables used in this book give the area in the *right* hand tail of the distribution). The calculation is as follows:

$$Z = \frac{805.5 - 800}{10} = 0.55$$

This gives an area of 0.2912 and area A is therefore $0.5 - 0.2912 = 0.2088$
    Area B is found in a similar manner.

$$Z = \frac{790 - 800}{10} = -1.0$$

The negative sign indicates that the area is to the left of the mean and can be ignored for the purposes of obtaining the area from the normal table. Area B is therefore

$$0.5 - 0.1587 = 0.3413.$$

The combined area is 0.2088 + 0.3413 = 0.5501 or 55.01%, which is the proportion of loaves with weights between 790g and 805.5g.

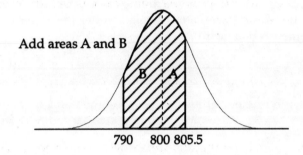

Add areas A and B

790   800 805.5

Figure 11

In addition to calculating the probability or proportion of a variable having a value between specified limits, it is possible to carry out the reverse process. This is illustrated in the next activity.

Activity 8

The baker wishes to ensure that no more than 5% of loaves are less than a certain weight. What is this weight?

The diagram for this problem can be seen in Figure 12 below. It is necessary to calculate the value 'x' but first the Z value corresponding to an area of 5% must be found. Although this area is in the lower tail, the method is identical to that used when the area in the upper tail has been given. (Don't forget the distribution is symmetrical about the mean). The value of Z for an area of 5% is 1.645 but because it is to the left of the mean, the value is negative, that is -1.645. Substituting this value into the formula gives:

$$-1.645 = \frac{x - 800}{10}$$

Multiplying both sides by 10 gives:

$$-16.45 = x - 800$$

Then adding 800 to both sides:

$$x = 800 - 16.45$$

$$= 783.6g$$

So no more than 5% of the batch should weigh less than 763.6g.

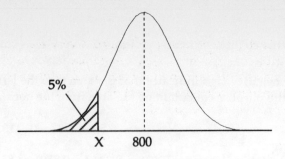

Figure 12

Although the preceding activities cover the most common applications, it is possible to use the Z formula to calculate either the mean or the standard deviation. This is demonstrated next.

Activity 9

A large number of loaves were weighed and it was found that 8% weighed less than 783.6g. Assuming that the standard deviation hasn't changed, what has happened?

This problem is illustrated in Figure 13 below. If the standard deviation hasn't changed then the only conclusion is that the mean has changed or it is not what it was thought to be. Again it is necessary to work backwards. The Z value corresponding to a proportion of 8% is 1.405, which will again be negative. The value of 'x' is 783.6 and it is required to find the value of the mean, μ.

$$-1.405 = \frac{783.6 - \mu}{10}$$

Multiplying both sides by 10, gives:

$$-14.05 = 783.6 - \mu$$

Then adding 14.05 to both sides:

$$0 = 797.7 - \mu$$

that is: $\mu = 797.7\text{g}$

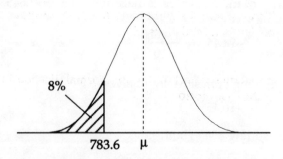

Figure 13

5.6 Summary

In this chapter you have examined a very important distribution called the normal distribution. You have seen how to use tables to obtain the area within the standard normal distribution and to obtain the Z value given the area. You have also seen how to transform a general normal distribution problem into the standard normal so that the problem can be solved.

5.7 Further reading

Morris, C, *Quantitative Approaches in Business Studies*, Pitman, 1993, Chapter 9

Harper, W, *Statistics, M & E Handbook Series*, Pitman, 1991, Chapter 18.

Booth, D.J, *A First Course in Statistics*, DP Publications, 1992, Chapter 6.

Oakshott, L, *Quantitative Approaches to Decision Making*, DP Publications, 1993, Unit 4.

5.8 Exercises

Progress questions

These question have been designed to help you remember the key points in this chapter. The answers to these questions are given in Appendix 1, page 134.

Give the missing word in each case:

1. The normal curve is .... about the mean.

2. The total area under the normal curve is ....

3. The position and shape of the normal curve is determined by the .... and ....

4. As the standard deviation gets larger the spread of the curve ....

5. The normal distribution is an example of a .... distribution.

Answer TRUE or FALSE

6. A Z value is a probability.

   True ☐ False ☐

7. The normal distribution is a 'bell' shape.

   True ☐ False ☐

8. If the area in the right hand tail of the normal distribution is 5%, then the area in the left hand tail is also 5%.

   True ☐ False ☐

9. If the area in each tail of the normal distribution is 5% then the area in the centre of the distribution is 95%.

   True ☐ False ☐

Review questions

These questions have been designed to help you check your comprehension of the key points in this chapter. You may wish to look further than this chapter in order to answer them fully. You will find the reading list useful in this respect. You can check the essential elements of your answers by referring to the appropriate section.

10. What are the properties of the normal distribution? (Section 5.3)

11. Why is it necessary to have a standard normal distribution and what is it? (Sections 5.4 and 5.5)

12. Give examples of data that may conform to the normal distribution. (Section 5.1)

Multiple choice questions

The answers to these will be given in the Lecturers' Supplement.

13. The standard normal distribution has a mean of
    A   0
    B   1
    C μ

14. The normal distribution is applicable to
    A   discrete data
    B   continuous data
    C   ordinal data

15. The distribution of weights of packets of biscuits is normal with a mean of 400g and a standard deviation of 10g. A packet was selected at random and found to weigh 420g. How many standard deviations away from the mean does this weight represent?
    A   10
    B   1
    C   2
    D   20

16. What proportion (approximately) of a normal distribution is covered by ±2 standard deviations?
    A   50%
    B   95%
    C   99%

Practice questions

Answers to these questions will be given in the Lecturers' Supplement.

17. What is the area in the tail of the distribution for a Z value of 1.25?

18. What is area between the Z values of 1.45 and 2.45?

19. What is the area between the Z value of -0.67 and 1.05?

20. A particular normal distribution has a mean of 5 and a standard deviation of 1.5. What is the area corresponding to a value:
    a) greater than 6
    b) less than 4
    c) between 4 and 6
    d) between 6.5 and 7.5

21. The daily demand for petrol at a garage is normally distributed with a mean of 20,000 litres and a standard deviation of 7200 litres. What is the probability that the demand in any one day is:

    a) greater than 25,000 litres

    b) greater than 17,000 litres

    c) between 20,000 and 25,000 litres

    d) between 30,000 and 35,000 litres

22. The length of a special type of bolt is normally distributed with a mean diameter of 5.5 mm and a standard deviation of 0.4mm. Bolts are only acceptable if their diameter is between 4.5 to 6 mm. What proportion of bolts will be accepted.

23. As an incentive for customers to spend more money on its credit card a bank has decided to award high spending customers with a free gift. However, it doesn't want to give gifts to more than 5% of customers. If the mean spend per customer is £135 with a standard deviation of £55, what balance should the company specify? However, at the end of the first month it was found that 8% of customers qualified for the free gift. What has happened? Assuming that the standard deviation hasn't changed calculate the new mean spend per customer.

Assignment:

Answers to this assignment are included in the Lecturers' Supplement.

Goodtaste Ltd a coffee manufacturer have recently been prosecuted for selling an underweight 100g jar of coffee. You have been asked to give assistance to the quality control manager who is investigating the problem.

Jars are filled automatically and the filling machine can be pre-set to any desired weight. For the 100g jars of coffee a weight of 101g is set. There is no subsequent checking of the weight of individual jars although samples are occasionally taken to check for quality. The standard deviation will depend to a certain extent on the mean weight but for weights between 90g to 110g it is virtually constant at 1.5g

You have been asked to apply your knowledge of the normal distribution to the problem. In particular you have been told that prosecution only occurs when the product is underweight by more than 2%, so you need to find the probability that such a weight could happen by chance.

a) Assuming that the mean weight is 101g, what proportion of jars are:

    i) under 100g in weight

    ii) under 98g in weight

    iii) under 97g in weight

    iv) over 100g

    v) within 2g of the marked weight.

b) What should the mean weight be set to in order that the probability of a jar weighing less than 98g is less than 0.1%?

c) Write a short note to the quality control manager summarising your results.

6 Analysis and interpretation of sample data

6.1 Introduction

You were introduced to the idea of sampling in Chapter 1. In that chapter the problems of recording information about the whole 'population' was discussed and the need for sampling became apparent. The population referred to in Chapter 1 was people and the purpose of sampling was to obtain reliable information about these people. This information could be concerned with income or their attitudes to a particular issue. In this chapter the population does not necessarily refer to people – it generally refers to data of any sort. So a quality control department may be interested in the mean weight of jars of coffee produced each day. Information from a sample is subject to error and the purpose of this chapter is to be able to quantify the accuracy of this information. This is achieved by stating the margin of error around the estimate of the population. This is called a confidence interval.

To complete this chapter successfully you should already have worked through Chapter 1 (Survey methods) and Chapter 5 (The Normal distribution).

On completing this chapter you should be able to:

❐ Obtain best estimates of the mean and standard deviation of a population.

❐ Calculate confidence intervals for a population mean.

❐ Calculate confidence intervals for a population percentage.

6.2 Samples and sampling

Sampling is an extensive and in many cases controversial technique. Whenever there is a general election in this country the question of sampling accuracy is raised and this was most evident in the 1992 election. However, sampling peoples views and intentions is notoriously difficult and even the best sampling plan can fail in these circumstances. Fortunately when sampling is done by measurement, the results tend to be much more reliable. Sampling in industry and business tends to be of the measurement kind and it will be this aspect of sampling that will be emphasised here.

Activity 1

Why is it necessary to take samples?

The alternative to taking samples is to measure or test every member of the 'population'. (The word population in this context doesn't necessarily mean people, it is used to define all the items or things that are of interest, such as all television sets produced by a company in a day). It is impractical to measure or test every member of the population for the following reasons:

❑ *It would take too long*. Measuring or testing can be time consuming and it is simply not always feasible to find the necessary time.

❑ *It is too expensive*. Testing costs money as inspectors need to be employed and goods that are to be tested take up space and cannot be sold until the testing is complete.

❑ *Some tests are destructive*. Sometimes goods have to be tested to destruction and if all the goods were tested there would be nothing left to sell!

❑ *The total population is unknown*. There are occasions when the size of the population is so large as to be considered infinite (without limit). In other cases the size of the population is simply unknown.

Activity 2

You work for a company that manufactures plastic containers. The raw material is supplied in granular form and is delivered in 100 kg bags. The granules have to be tested for fire resistance and you are given the job of selecting the material for testing. How would you go about this task?

Since this is likely to be destructive testing, the only option available to you is to test a sample from each consignment. It is important that more than one bag is tested since one particular bag may not be typical of the rest of the batch. Perhaps this bag happens to be old stock or is different in some way. Whenever you take samples you must ensure that the samples are selected at random; that is every member of the population has an equal chance of being selected. (See Chapter 1). In this case you would need to randomly select a number of bags and then test a small quantity from each of the bags selected. The number of bags chosen and the amount of material tested from each bag would depend on the specific requirements of the test.

6.3 Point estimates

The whole purpose of obtaining a sample from a population is to obtain estimates of various population parameters such as the mean, the standard deviation or percentage. These parameters can also be obtained for the sample and it is the purpose of this section to show how the population parameters and the sample parameters are related. However, before continuing, it is necessary to define the symbols that are to be used throughout this (and the next) chapter.

The convention is to use Greek letters for the population parameters and normal letters for the sample parameters. The various symbols used are given below.

Parameter	Population	Sample
Mean	μ	$\bar{x}$
Standard deviation	σ	S
Percentage	π	P

The one exception to this rule is that the size of the population is usually referred to as '*N*' and the sample size as '*n*'.

Example 1

10 samples of plastic granules were tested for fire resistance and the combustion temperature (in centigrade) are as follows:

Sample No.	1	2	3	4	5	6	7	8	9	10
Temperature	510	535	498	450	491	505	487	500	501	469

Activity 3

What is the mean and standard deviation of these figures in Example 1 and what can you conclude about the whole batch?

You should have found the mean to be 494.6°C with a standard deviation of 21.85°C. (See Chapter 3, page 34 if you are not sure about these calculations). You will probably not be surprised to learn that the 'best' (or unbiased) estimate of the population mean is $\bar{x}$. Therefore the best estimate of the mean of the batch is 494.6°C. But what is the best estimate of the population standard deviation? It is not S, the sample standard deviation as S is an *underestimate* of the true figure. To understand this, imagine that the population of temperatures follows some probability distribution. This distribution has a few extreme values but most of them are clustered around the mean. The population standard deviation is a measure of spread and all values, including the extreme ones, contribute to this value. However, if a sample is chosen at random the sample is most unlikely to include any of the extreme values and therefore the spread and hence the standard deviation of the sample will be less than the population. You should also realise that as the sample gets larger, the standard deviation will get closer and closer to the population value since the chance of selecting an extreme value increases.

So how is σ calculated? Fortunately there is quite a simple formula relating S and σ, it is as follows:

$$\sigma = S\sqrt{\frac{n}{n-1}}$$

This is known as Bessel's correction factor.

You will see that as n gets larger the factor under the square root gets closer to 1, which ties in with the discussion above. For 'large' samples, which is generally considered to be anything above 30, this correction is usually ignored.

For the plastic granules, the estimate of the population standard deviation is:

$$\sigma = 21.85 \times \sqrt{\frac{10}{9}}$$
$$= 23.03$$

6.4 Sampling distribution of the means

Imagine that you took lots and lots of samples and calculated the mean of each. Each mean is an estimate of the population value and therefore the 'mean of the means' should be an even better estimate. If you now plotted the distribution of the means, what shape would you expect the distribution to be? The answer is that the shape would tend towards the *normal* curve. The degree of agreement with the normal curve depends on two factors:

❏ the distribution of the population values;

❏ the sample size.

If the population values are normally distributed, the 'sampling distribution of the means' would also be normal. If the population is not normally distributed the agreement with the normal distribution depends on the sample size; the larger the sample size, the closer the agreement. This very important result is known as the *central limit theorem*.

In addition, the spread of this sampling distribution depends on the sample size; the larger the sample size, the smaller the spread (that is, the standard deviation). The standard deviation of the sampling distribution is called the standard error as it measures the error that could arise in your estimate due to the spread of the sampling distribution. To avoid confusion with the standard error of the sampling distribution of a percentage, which will be discussed later (page 93), the standard error of the sampling distribution of the means will be referred to as *STEM* (the *ST*andard *E*rror of the *M*eans). Is it necessary to collect many samples in order to calculate the value of STEM? Fortunately not, as there is a relationship between σ and STEM. This relationship is as follows:

$$STEM = \frac{\sigma}{\sqrt{n}}$$

So the larger the sample size (n), the smaller the value of STEM, which makes sense.

These ideas are illustrated in Figure 1, below. Two sampling distributions are shown, one for a sample size of 4 and one for a sample size of 16. The population distribution (assumed normal in this case) has been superimposed onto the diagram.

Sampling distribution of the means

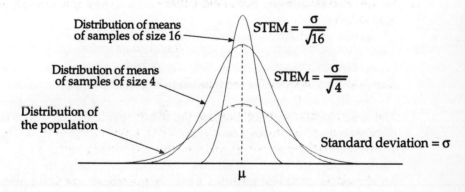

Figure 1

You will see that the mean of each sampling distribution is the same and equal to the population value. You would normally only take one sample and from Figure 1 you can see that the mean of a sample can lie anywhere within the relevant sampling distribution; although it is more likely to be near the centre than in the tails. This variation depends on the value of STEM, so the smaller this figure, the more reliable your estimate of the population mean will be.

The value of STEM when n=10 is:

$$\text{STEM} = \frac{23.75}{\sqrt{10}}$$

$$= \frac{23.75}{3.1623}$$

$$= 7.510$$

That is 7.510°C. When n=40 STEM becomes:

$$\text{STEM} = \frac{23.75}{\sqrt{40}}$$

$$= \frac{23.75}{6.3246}$$

$$= 3.755$$

That is 3.755°C. Notice that to half the value of STEM, the sample size was increased fourfold. Calculation of the sample size necessary to give a prescribed level of accuracy will be discussed later (page 93).

6.5 Confidence intervals for a population mean using the normal distribution

Rather than simply quote the value of STEM, a much better idea of the reliability of your estimate is to specify some limits within which the true mean is expected to lie. These limits are called confidence limits or intervals.

When calculating confidence intervals it is necessary to decide what level of confidence you wish to use. The most common level is 95%, which means that you are 95% confident that the true mean lies within the calculated limits. Or put another way, there is a 5% chance that the true mean doesn't lie within these limits. Other limits are frequently used, such as 90%, 99% and 99.9%; but remember that as the confidence level gets closer to 100%, the interval gets larger and larger (at 100% it would be infinitely large).

The *normal distribution* (see Chapter 5, page 74) can be used to calculate these limits if the population is normal and the standard deviation of the population (σ) is known. If normality cannot be assumed then a large sample size will ensure that the sampling distribution of the means is approximately normal.

However, in the many situations σ is unknown and has to be estimated from the sample. In these cases the normal distribution can be used as an approximation, provided the sample size is large. Alternatively the 't-distribution' can be used (this will be discussed later).

Figure 2 below, illustrates the Z values that enclose 95% of the standard normal distribution (see page 77). The values ±1.96 have been found from the normal table (Appendix 2, page 135) by noting that the area (or probability) in either tail is $.025 = \frac{0.05}{2}$.

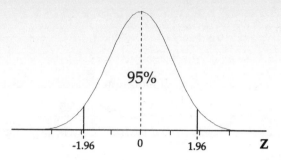

Figure 2 95% Confidence intervals

From your knowledge of the normal distribution, you will know that any normal distribution can be transformed into the standard normal distribution using the formula:

$$Z = \frac{x - \mu}{\sigma}$$

However, this formula is for individual 'x' values. For a sampling distribution of the means, the 'x' needs to be replaced by $\bar{x}$ and σ needs to be replaced by STEM. The formula then becomes:

$$Z = \frac{\bar{x} - \mu}{\text{STEM}}$$

If you rearrange this formula to make μ the subject, you will get:

$$\mu = \bar{x} \pm z \times \text{STEM}$$

This is the equation you would use to calculate confidence intervals using the normal distribution. For 95% confidence intervals the Z value is 1.96 and the formula becomes:

$$\mu = \bar{x} \pm 1.96 \times \text{STEM}$$

How would you use this formula? The next example should help you.

Example 2

Imagine that you worked for the quality control unit of a sugar producer. One of your tasks is to weigh samples of 1 kg bags of sugar and from a sample of 6 bags you obtain a mean weight of 0.958 kg.

Activity 5

You know from previous investigations that the weights of individual bags of sugar are normally distributed with a standard deviation of 0.056 kg. What is the 95% confidence interval for the true mean weight of bags of sugar?

From the discussion on point estimates (page 87), you know that the best estimate of the true mean is 0.958 kg. That is:

$$\mu = 0.958 \text{ kg}$$

From this you can assume that the best estimate of the mean of the sampling distribution for a sample size 6 also has this value. The value of STEM is:

$$\frac{\sigma}{\sqrt{n}} = \frac{0.056}{\sqrt{6}}$$

$$= 0.02286$$

Therefore the 95% confidence interval for the true mean is:

$$0.958 \pm 1.96 \times 0.02286 \;\; = 0.958 \pm 0.045$$

$$= 0.958 - 0.045 \text{ and } 0.958 + 0.045$$

$$= 0.913 \text{ and } 1.003 \text{ kg}$$

The 0.913 kg is the *lower* limit and 1.003 kg is the *upper* limit. The 0.045 is often called the *half width* of the confidence interval. It is usual to write this confidence interval as:

$$0.913, 1.003 \text{ (or } 0.913 \text{ to } 1.003)$$

This interval is summarised in the diagram below:

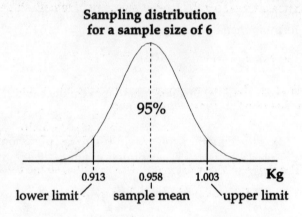

Figure 3

Notice that the interval includes 1 kg, so this may indicate that the process is producing bags of sugar with a mean weight of 1 kg. But more about this later (Chapter7).

If accuracy was really important you may want to calculate 99% confidence intervals. From the normal table, the value of Z for 0.005 (1% divided by 2) is 2.58, so the 99% confidence interval is:

$$0.958 \pm 2.58 \times 0.02286 \;\; = 0.958 \pm 0.059$$

$$= 0.899, 1.017 \text{ kg}$$

The interval is wider, which was expected. Now there is only a 1% chance that the true mean will be outside these limits. If these limits are too wide the only way to reduce them (for the same confidence level) is to increase the sample size (see page 93).

6.6 *Confidence interval of a percentage*

Percentages occur quite frequently in the analysis of survey results. For example, the percentage of people who like a particular product or the percentage of students over the age of 25. Provided n is large and the percentage is not too small or too large, the sampling distribution of a percentage can be approximated by the normal distribution.

The standard error of the sampling distribution of percentages (STEP) is:

$$STEP = \sqrt{\frac{P(100 - P)}{n}}$$

where P is the sample percentage

The calculation of a confidence interval for a percentage is similar to that of the mean, that is:

$$\pi = P \pm Z \times STEP$$

Activity 6

A survey among 250 students revealed that 147 were female. What is the 95% confidence interval for the true percentage of female students?

The value of P is $\frac{147}{250} \times 100 = 58.8\%$.

That is, the survey suggested that 58.8% of the student population is female. The value of STEP for this problem is:

$$\sqrt{\frac{58.8 \times (100 - 58.8)}{250}} = 3.113$$

The value of Z for 95% confidence is 1.96, so the confidence interval becomes:

$$58.8 \pm 1.96 \times 3.113 \ = 58.8 \pm 6.1$$

$$= 52.7, 64.9$$

That is, the true percentage lies somewhere between 52.7% to 64.9%.

6.7 Calculation of sample size

Since the value of both STEM and STEP depend on the sample size, the width of the confidence interval for the same confidence level, can be reduced by increasing the value of 'n'. For the sugar example (Example 2) the half width of the interval, that is, the difference between the lower or upper limit and the sample mean, is 0.045 kg for a confidence level of 95%. This was obtained by multiplying STEM by 1.96, that is:

Half width of confidence interval $= 1.96 \times STEM$

$$= 1.96 \times \frac{\sigma}{\sqrt{n}}$$

If you wanted to reduce this half width to say, 0.025 kg, then you need to calculate the value of n required to achieve this reduction. That is:

$$1.96 \times \frac{0.056}{\sqrt{n}} = 0.025$$

since $\sigma = 0.056$ (see Activity 5).

Re-arranging this equation gives:

$$\sqrt{n} = \frac{1.96 \times 0.056}{0.025}$$

$$= 4.3904$$

To remove the square root you have to *square* it and if you square the left hand side of an equation you must square the right hand side as well. This gives:

$$n = 19.3$$

So a sample size of 20 would be required to achieve an accuracy of ±0.025 kg.

Activity 7

What sample size would be required to reduce the half width for the percentage of female students from 6.1% to 1%?

The calculation is similar to that for the mean. That is:

$$1.96 \times STEP = 1.0$$

The value of P is 58.8% (see page 93), so:

$$1.96 \times \sqrt{\frac{58.8 \times (100 - 58.8)}{n}} = 1.0$$

Dividing both sides by 1.96 and squaring gives:

$$\frac{58.8 \times 41.2}{n} = 0.2603$$

Therefore:

$$n = \frac{58.8 \times 41.2}{0.2603}$$

$$= 9306.8$$

That is, a sample of about 9000 students would need to be selected to ensure this level of accuracy!

6.8 Confidence intervals for a population mean using the t-distribution

If the standard deviation of the population is *not* known, it could be estimated from the sample using Bessel's correction factor (page 88). However, in this case you would not generally be justified in using the normal table. The reason for this is that the uncertainty generated by estimating σ decreases the reliability of the confidence interval. To overcome this problem a different distribution is used, called the '*t-distribution*'. This distribution is symmetrical like the normal, but it is flatter. This 'flatness' increases the percentage of the distribution in the 'tails' and this means that the confidence interval, for the same confidence level, is wider. The amount of 'flatness' decreases with increase in '*n*', the sample size. When '*n*' is 50 there is virtually no difference between the two distributions and even for a sample size of 30 the difference is quite small. This similarity between the two distributions allows you to use the normal distribution for large samples. Many authors suggest that 30 is the cut-off figure. However, you should remember that the use of the normal distribution in these cases is an approximation.

Figure 4 below, shows the t-distribution for a sample size of 6 together with the normal distribution for comparison.

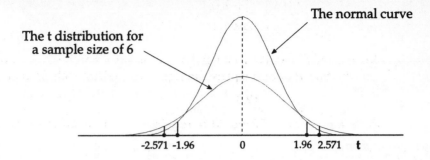

Figure 4 *Comparison of the normal and t-distributions*

The *t* table is given in Appendix 2, page 136. If you compare this table with the normal table, you will see some important differences. For a start, the numbers within the table are *t*-values and not probabilities. The other difference is the numbers in the first column. These numbers are the '*degrees of freedom*' (df) of the sample. Degrees of freedom can be thought of as the 'freedom' that you have in choosing the values of the sample. If you were given the mean of the sample of 6 values, you would be free to choose 5 of the 6 but not the sixth one. Therefore there are 5 degrees of freedom. *The number of degrees of freedom for a single sample of size 'n' is 'n–1'.* For a very large sample (shown as ∞ in the table) the *t* and Z distributions are exactly the same. Since the t-distribution is a little easier to use, you might prefer to use this table when you want the Z value of one of the 'standard' probabilities. In the table supplied in this book these 'standard' probabilities are 0.2, 0.1, 0.05, 0.025, 0.01, 0.005, 0.001 and 0.0001.

To use this table you would first decide on the probability level. For a 95% confidence interval you would choose the 0.025 level since this represents 2.5% in each tail. For a sample size of 6, the degrees of freedom is 5, so the *t* value for 5 degrees of freedom at 95% confidence level is 2.571. This value has been shown in Figure 4. (Remember that the *t*-distribution is symmetrical about the mean of zero, so the equivalent value in the left hand side of the distribution is –2.571).

The formula for calculating confidence intervals using this distribution is the same as when the normal distribution was used except that 'Z' is replaced by '*t*' and is therefore:

$$\mu = \bar{x} \pm t \times \text{STEM}$$

Activity 8

In Activity 3 you calculated the mean and standard deviation of the combustion temperatures of a sample of size 10 to be 494.6°C and 21.85°C respectively. Calculate the 95% confidence intervals for true mean combustion temperature of the entire batch.

The best estimate of σ was 23.03°C (see page 88) so the value of STEM is:

$$\frac{23.03}{\sqrt{10}} = 7.283$$

To find the 95% confidence interval for the true mean you would use the t table in Appendix 2 to find the appropriate value of t. The value of t for 9 degrees of freedom, with a probability of 0.025 is 2.262. Substituting this value into the equation for μ gives you:

$$494.6 \pm 2.262 \times 7.283 \quad = 494.6 \pm 16.5$$

$$= 478.1, 511.1°C$$

So the true mean combustion temperature of the whole consignment lies between 478.1 to 511.1°C at the 95% level of confidence.

6.9 Finite Populations

The assumption that has implicitly been made in this chapter is that the population is infinitely large, or at least much larger than the sample. The reason for this is that all sampling is done without replacement. That is, you would not measure or test the same person or item twice. This has no effect when the population is large, but for small populations, the probability that an item will be selected will change as soon as one item has been selected. (See conditional probability, page 58). To overcome this problem, the standard error (either STEM or STEP) is modified. This is achieved by multiplying the value by the *Finite Population Correction Factor*, which is:

$$\sqrt{\frac{N-n}{N-1}}$$

Where N is the size of the population.

Activity 9

In the sugar example (Example 2) STEM was 0.02286 (see page 92). What is the value of STEM if the size of the population was 100.

The value of STEM is multiplied by the correction factor, that is:

$$0.02286 \times \sqrt{\frac{100-6}{100-1}} \quad = 0.02286 \times 0.9744$$

$$= 0.02228$$

which is a reduction. (Since STEM is reduced, confidence intervals will also be reduced).

As 'N' gets larger relative to 'n', the correction factor approaches 1 and can therefore be ignored. For example, if you try $N = 10,000$ and $n = 10$, you should get a value of 0.9995.

6.10 Summary

In this chapter you were introduced to the idea of the central limit theorem. This is one of the most important theorems in statistics and allows you to make inferences about a population from a sample. By knowing that the sampling distribution follows the normal distribution allows you to calculate the interval within which the population mean or percentage is likely to lie. These intervals are called confidence intervals and allow you to specify the confidence you have with the calculated interval.

6.11 Further reading

Morris, C, *Quantitative Approaches in Business Studies*, Pitman, 1993, Chapter 10

Oakshott, L, *Quantitative Approaches to Decision Making*, DP Publications, 1993, Unit 6.

Lucey, T, *Quantitative Techniques*, DP Publications, 1992, Chapter 5.

6.12 Exercises

Progress questions

These question have been designed to help you remember the key points in this chapter. The answers to these questions are given in Appendix 1, page 134.

Give the missing word in each case.

1. All items of interest is called a ....

2. A subset of all items of interest is called a ....

3. A single estimate of some variable of interest is called a .... estimate.

4. The best estimate of the true mean is the .... mean.

5. The standard deviation of a sample is .... than the true figure.

6. An interval estimate is also known as a .... interval.

Answer TRUE or FALSE

7. The Z table is only used when the sample size is large.

    True ☐ False ☐

8. The t-distribution approaches the normal distribution as the sample size increases.

    True ☐ False ☐

9. It is necessary to be given the standard deviation of the population for the t-distribution to be used.

    True ☐ False ☐

10. As the sample size increases the error in your estimate decreases.

    True ☐ False ☐

11. For small samples a t-distribution must be used.

    True ☐ False ☐

12. The use of the normal distribution to calculate confidence intervals for a percentage is only an approximation.

    True ☐ False ☐

13. If the sample size doubles the half width of the confidence interval reduces by a half.

     True ☐ False ☐

14. A 95% confidence interval means that 95% of samples will have a mean or percentage within this interval.

     True ☐ False ☐

Review questions

These questions have been designed to help you check your comprehension of the key points in this chapter. You may wish to look further than this chapter in order to answer them fully. You will find the reading list useful in this respect. You can check the essential elements of your answers by referring to the appropriate section.

15. Why is it necessary to take samples? (Section 6.2)

16. Explain the importance of the central limit theorem to statistics. (Section 6.4)

17. Describe the essential differences between the normal and the t-distributions (Sections 6.5 and 6.8)

18. What effect does sample size have on a confidence interval? (Section 6.7)

19. What effect does a small population have on a confidence interval? (Section 6.9)

Multiple choice questions

The answers to these will be given in the Lecturers' Supplement.

Questions 20 to 23 refer to the sample 34.5, 25.7, 20.1, 38.9, 33.0, 33.2, 22.8 and 30.5 denoted by 'X'. This sample was taken from a large population denoted by 'P'.

20. The mean of 'X' (to 2 decimal places) is:
    A   25.26   B   29.84   C   39.55

21. The standard deviation of 'X' (to 2 decimal places) is:
    A   5.99   B   6.40   C   25.26

22. The best estimate of the standard deviation of 'P' is.
    A   5.99   B   6.40   C   25.26

23. The value of STEM is:
    A   2.26   B   2.12   C   5.99

24. The sampling distribution of the means follows a:
    A   uniform distribution
    B   normal distribution
    C   empirical distribution
    D t-distribution

25. The standard deviation of the sampling distribution of the means is called:
    A STEM
    B STEP
    C σ
    D μ

26. The standard deviation of the sampling distribution of a percentage is called:
    A STEM
    B STEP
    C σ
    D μ

Practice questions

Answers to these questions will be given in the Lecturers' Supplement.

27. A university contains 16,000 students and it is required to find out how many students have part time jobs. 50 students are selected at random and of these 20 admitted to working during term time. What is the value of the:
    a) Population   b) sample   c) sample percentage
    d) estimate of the true percentage
    e) 95% confidence interval of the true percentage

28. A sample of six packets of tea is selected from a production line. The contents of these packets are 9.4, 9.1, 10.2, 8.9, 10.9 and 9.2 grams respectively. Obtain the 95% confidence interval estimate of the mean net weight of a packet, if the standard deviation is known to be 0.79g.

29. A random sample of 100 adult females from the population of a large town has a mean height of 169.5 cm with a standard deviation of 2.6 cm. Construct a 95% Confidence Interval for the mean height of all adult females in the town.

30. A sample of 60 people were asked if they thought that if children watched video 'nasties' they more likely to commit a crime. Out of the sample, 45 thought that they would. Calculate the 95% confidence interval for the true percentage.

31. The weight of each of 10 specimens of carbon paper were found to be (in grams):

    7.4, 8.3, 10.9, 6.9, 7.9, 8.2, 8.6, 9.1, 9.9, 10.0

    Given that the weights are normally distributed construct (a) 95% and (b) 99% confidence interval for μ, the true mean of the population weights.

32. A credit card company wants to determine the mean income of its card holders. A random sample of 225 card holders was drawn and the sample average income was £16,450 with a sample standard deviation of £3,675.
    i) Construct a 99% confidence interval for the true mean income.
    ii) Management decided that the confidence interval in (i) was too large to be useful. In particular the management wanted to estimate the mean income to within £200 with a confidence level of 99%. How large a sample should be selected?

33. From a population of 200, a sample of 40 people were asked for their views on capital punishment. 12 people thought that hanging should be imposed for certain crimes. Estimate the 95% confidence interval for the true percentage.

Assignment

Answers to this assignment are included in the Lecturers' supplement.

The latest internal accounts for an off licence chain showed that the annual sales of wines and spirits had fallen by more than 30%. This fall has been blamed on the relaxation of the limits of duty free goods that can be brought into Britain from EEC countries from 1993.

In order to test this theory it was decided to ask a random sample of shoppers if they intend to travel to France this year. Of the 75 shoppers questioned, 27 were certain to go to France at least once. It was also decided to ask a random sample of 60 returning holiday makers how much they had spent on duty free alcohol. Of these 60, eight refused to answer and for the remaining 52 people the average spend was found to be £37.26 with a standard deviation of £35.97.

i) What is the percentage of shoppers who said they were definitely making at least one trip to France this year?

ii) Calculate the 95% confidence interval for the true percentage of shoppers who intend to travel to France this year? Interpret this interval.

iii) Calculate the 95% confidence interval for the true mean amount spent spend on duty free alcohol for all holiday makers returning from France.

iv) Calculate the number of shoppers to be questioned so that the 'half width' of the confidence interval is no more than 3%.

v) The half width of the confidence interval for the average spend on duty free alcohol wants to be reduced to £5. How many holiday makers need to be sampled?

vi) What reservations (if any) do you have about this kind of survey?

7 Testing a hypothesis

7.1 Introduction

In Chapter 6 you saw how to analyse a sample so that estimates of some population parameter, such as the mean or percentage, could be obtained. In this chapter the emphasis is slightly different in that you are told the value of some population parameter and then use the sample to confirm or disprove this figure. For example, you may want to determine the effects on fuel consumption of a particular make of car by modification to the carburation system or you may want to determine if a union can be sure that if a ballot was called the majority of the membership would vote for strike action. In both these examples a hypothesis would be made concerning the population and this hypothesis tested using the sample data.

To complete this chapter successfully you should have read through Chapter 6 (Analysis and interpretation of sample data).

On completing this chapter you should be able to:

❏ Understand the ideas behind hypothesis testing

❏ Perform tests of hypothesis on a mean of a population

❏ Perform tests of hypothesis on a percentage

❏ Carry out a 'goodness-of-fit' test

❏ Apply the Chi squared test to categorical data

7.2 The purpose of hypothesis testing

Activity 1

The light bulbs manufactured by 'Bright Lights' are designed to last for 1000 hours on average. How can the company be sure that the average lifetime of a large batch of bulbs really is 1000 hours?

The mean lifetime could be found by testing a sample of bulbs and constructing a confidence interval within which the true mean is likely to lie. If the interval does contain 1000 hours, then you could assume that the true mean really is 1000 hours.

Alternatively, you could construct a confidence interval for the supposed true mean of 1000 hours and see if the sample mean was contained within this interval.

However, there is a third approach. This approach makes the hypothesis that any departure from the supposed true mean by the sample mean is simply due to chance effects. It is then a matter of calculating the probability that this sample result could have occurred by chance. This is the general idea of hypothesis testing- it assumes that the hypothesis is true and then tries to disprove it. This hypothesis is known as the *null* hypothesis. If the null hypothesis is rejected an *alternative* hypothesis is accepted. The null hypothesis is called 'H_0' and the alternative hypothesis 'H_1'.

The null hypothesis is tested at a particular *significance level*. This level relates to the area (or probability) in the tail of the distribution being used for the test. This area is called the *critical region* and if the test statistic lies in the critical region, you would infer that the result is unlikely to have occurred by chance. You would then reject the null hypothesis. For example, if the 5% level of significance was used and the null hypothesis was rejected, you would say that H_0 had been rejected at the 5% (or the 0.05) significance level, and the result was *significant*.

These ideas apply to all types of hypothesis tests. The precise form of each hypothesis and the calculations necessary to test H_0 depend on the test being carried out. There are very many tests that can be applied to samples. The most important group are *parametric* tests. These tests compare sample statistics with the population parameters and make assumptions about the form of the sampling distribution. *Non-parametric* (or distribution-free) tests are more general and do not insist on such stringent conditions. They can also be used where the data can only be ordered (ordinal data) rather than measured. However non-parametric tests are less discriminating; that is, the results tend to be less reliable.

Whatever the test, the steps for checking the hypothesis are the same. These are:

Step 1. Set up the null and alternative hypotheses and determine (usually from tables) the boundaries of the critical region. These boundaries are called the critical values.

Step 2. Calculate the test statistic

Step 3. Decide whether to accept or reject H_0

7.3 The Z test for a sample mean

The normal distribution can be used to solve problems involving means if the population is normal *and* the standard deviation of the population (σ) is known. If normality cannot be assumed then a large sample size will ensure that the sampling distribution of the means is approximately normal.

However, as in the calculation of confidence intervals (see Chapter 6, page 86) σ may be unknown and has to be estimated from the sample. In these cases the normal distribution can be used as an approximation, provided the sample size is large. Alternatively the '*t-test*' can be used (this will be discussed later).

The formula for 'Z' is also the same as that used in the derivation of the formula for confidence intervals. That is:

$$Z = \frac{\bar{x} - \mu}{\text{STEM}}$$

where $\bar{x}$ is the mean of the sample, μ is the mean of the population and STEM is the standard error of the sampling distribution of the means and is given by:

$$\text{STEM} = \frac{\sigma}{\sqrt{n}}$$

where 'n' is the sample size.

Activity 2

The distribution of the lifetime of all bulbs made by Bright Lights is normal and the standard deviation of the population is known to be 120 hours. A sample of 15 bulbs were tested and the mean lifetime was found to be 1100 hours, is this consistent, at the 5% level of significance, with the supposed true mean of 1000 hours?

Step 1:   Set up H_0 and H_1 and decide on the critical values

The null hypothesis in this case is that the true mean lifetime is 1000 hours. The alternative hypothesis can be one of three statements. These are:

The true mean is *not* equal to 1000 hours

or   The true mean is greater than 1000 hours

or   The true mean is less than 1000 hours.

Using symbols, the null and alternative hypotheses become:

$H_0: \mu = 1000$ hours $H_1: \mu \neq 1000$ hours

or $H_1: \mu > 1000$ hours

or $H_1: \mu < 1000$ hours

(The ':' is the mathematical shorthand for 'such that')

The first form of the alternative hypothesis is used for a *two tailed* (or a two sided) test and the other two forms are used for one tailed tests. The two tailed test is used when you have no reason to suppose that the true mean could be either greater than or less than the value given by the null hypothesis. The one tailed test is used when you are more interested in one side of the supposed mean than the other. The golden rule when carrying out hypothesis tests is that H_0 and H_1 are set up before the test is carried out (and preferably *before* the data is collected). You may find the diagrams below helpful in clarifying the situation.

Two tailed test at the 5% significance level

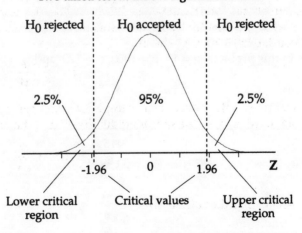

Figure 1

In Figure 1 the critical values of ± 1.96 mark the boundaries of the two critical regions at the 5% significance level. These values are found from the normal table in Appendix 2, page 135. If the test statistic (Z) is either greater than the right hand critical value or less than the left hand value, then H_0 is rejected. If Z lies in between the two critical values then H_0 is accepted – *or you should really say that you do not have sufficient information to reject H_0.*

One tailed tests for the 5% significance level

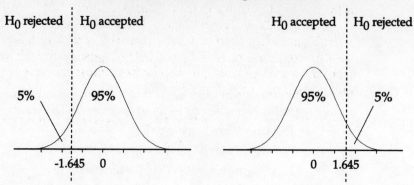

Figure 2

The left hand diagram of Figure 2 illustrates the case where the alternative hypothesis is of the 'less than' kind. There is only one critical region in this case and you would reject H_0 if Z was less than the critical value of –1.645. The reason that the critical value is different than for the two tailed case is that the area in the one tail is now the full amount (5% in this example) and not half as it was before. The right hand diagram is for the 'greater than' case and the same reasoning applies here as in the left hand diagram. That is, H_0 would be rejected if Z was *greater* than 1.645.

The light bulb example would be a two tailed test because there is nothing in the wording of the problem that suggests that you are more interested in one side of the mean. So the null and alternative hypothesis for this example are:

$$H_0: \mu = 1000 \text{ hours} \qquad H_1: \mu \neq 1000 \text{ hours}$$

and the critical values are ± 1.96

Step 2: Calculate the test statistic

In this problem, $n = 15$, $\mu = 1000$, $\sigma = 120$, and $\bar{x} = 1100$.

Therefore:
$$\text{STEM} = \frac{\sigma}{\sqrt{n}}$$

$$= \frac{120}{\sqrt{15}}$$

$$= 30.9839$$

and:
$$Z = \frac{\bar{x} - \mu}{\sqrt{n}}$$

$$= \frac{1100 - 1000}{30.9839}$$

$$= \frac{100}{30.9839}$$

$$= 3.23$$

This is your test statistic.

Step 3: Decide whether to accept or reject H_0

It is now necessary to decide if this value of Z could have happened by chance or if it is indicative of a change in the population mean.

Since Z (3.23) is greater than 1.96 and is therefore in the critical region, you can reject H_0 at the 5% level of significance. This is shown clearly in Figure 3 below where the 0.1% significance level (Z = 3.091) has also been added. The result is significant and you would conclude that there has almost certainly been a change in the mean lifetime of light bulbs.

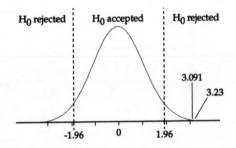

Figure 3

The following activity illustrates the use of one tailed tests.

Activity 3

The mean fuel consumption for a particular make of car is known to be 33 mpg with a standard deviation of 5.7 mpg. A modification to this car has been made that should reduce fuel consumption. 35 cars are fitted with this device and their fuel consumption is recorded over 12 months. At the end of this period the mean fuel consumption of the 35 cars is found to be 34.8 mpg. Is there any evidence, at the 5% level of significance, that the fuel consumption has been improved?

This is a one tailed test since is hoped that the modification will improve the fuel consumption- there is nothing to suggest that fuel consumption will be made worse. The Z test can be used without assuming normality because the sample is 'large' (over 30).

The null and alternative hypotheses for this problem are:

$$H_0: \mu = 33 \text{ mpg} \quad H_1: \mu > 33 \text{ mpg}$$

And the critical value of Z at the 5% significance level is 1.645

$$\sigma = 5.7 \text{ mpg}, \quad \bar{x} = 34.8 \text{ mpg} \quad \text{and } n = 35$$

Therefore:
$$\text{STEM} = \frac{5.7}{\sqrt{35}}$$
$$= 0.9635$$

and the test statistic:
$$Z = \frac{34.8 - 33.0}{0.9635}$$
$$= 1.868$$

Since 1.868 is greater than the critical value of 1.645, you would reject the null hypothesis. That is, there is a *significant* difference between the mean fuel consumption before and after the modification has been fitted. You would conclude that the modification appears to have improved the fuel consumption of this particular make of car.

It is important to draw a diagram when carrying out hypothesis tests. The diagram for this problem is shown below.

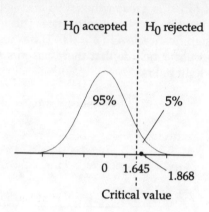

H_0 accepted H_0 rejected

95%   5%

0   1.645   1.868

Critical value

Figure 4

This diagram clearly shows that the test statistic is in the critical region and H_0 should therefore be rejected. You may have noticed that H_0 would not have been rejected if the test had been two tailed. (Compare this diagram with Figure 1). This is why it is so important to ensure that you are justified in using a one tailed test as the chance of rejecting H_0 is greater in the one tailed case.

7.4 The Z test for a sample percentage

Testing a sample percentage against some expected or hypothesised value (π) is another important test. The test given here is based on the assumption that 'n' is large and π is not too large or too small.

The standard error of the sampling distribution of a percentage (STEP) was given in Chapter 6 as:

$$\sqrt{\frac{P(100 - P)}{n}}$$

where P is the sample percentage.

However, for hypothesis testing it is the population parameter, π that must be used. With this substitution, the equation for STEP becomes:

$$STEP = \sqrt{\frac{\pi(100 - \pi)}{n}}$$

The Z statistic is similar to that used for the test on a mean and is:

$$Z = \frac{P - \pi}{STEP}$$

The following activity illustrates how the test would be carried out.

Activity 4

A trade union is considering strike action and intends to ballot its large membership on the issue. In order to gauge the likely result of the ballot, a survey was conducted among a random sample of members. Of the 60 people surveyed, 36 were in favour of a strike. Would the ballot give the required majority for a strike?

For a strike to be called, at least 50% of the membership must agree. Anything less would not be good enough. The null and alternative hypothesis should therefore be:

$$H_0: \pi = 50\% \quad H_1: \pi > 50\%$$

The cut-off point for the decision is a percentage of 50% and the test will determine if the sample percentage (p) of $\dfrac{36}{60} \times 100 = 60\%$ is significantly *greater* than 50%.

The critical value for a one tailed test at the 5% level is 1.645.

So:
$$\text{STEP} = \sqrt{\frac{50 \times (100 - 50)}{60}}$$
$$= 6.455$$

and the test statistic:
$$Z = \frac{60 - 50}{6.455}$$
$$= 1.549$$

Since 1.549 is less than 1.645, H_0 cannot be rejected. That is, it appears that there will not be a majority for strike action. However, the critical value and test statistic are quite close, and therefore the result is hardly conclusive. (Don't forget that the survey result is only a 'snapshot' of people's opinion at one instant in time. Some people may not have been entirely honest with their answers and others may change their opinion before the ballot.)

Figure 5 below confirms that the test statistic is just in the acceptance region.

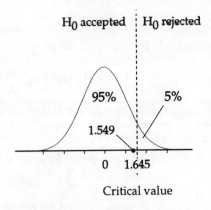

Figure 5

7.5 The t-test for a sample mean

As in the case of confidence intervals, the normal distribution is only an approximation when the standard deviation of the population has to be estimated from the sample. In this case the t-distribution should be used, particularly if the sample size is small. The formula for the t *statistic* is:

$$t = \frac{\bar{x} - \mu}{\text{STEM}}$$

Which is identical to the expression for Z. The formula for STEM is also the same, except that the standard deviation used is the estimate obtained from the sample. That is:

$$\text{STEM} = \frac{\sigma}{\sqrt{n}}$$

The same considerations apply concerning the critical region, except that the critical value is obtained from the t-distribution on n–1 degrees of freedom (Appendix 2, page 136). For example, the critical value on 7 degrees of freedom at the 5% significance level is ±2.365 for a two tailed test and ±1.895 for a one tailed test.

The following activity may help you understand the differences between the Z and t tests.

Activity 5

A tomato grower has developed a new variety of tomato. This variety is supposed to give good crops without the need for a greenhouse. One of the supposed attributes of this tomato is that the average yield per plant is 4 kg of fruit. A gardening magazine decides to test this claim and grows 8 plants in controlled conditions. The yield from each plant is carefully recorded and is as follows:

Plant:	1	2	3	4	5	6	7	8
Yield	3.6	4.2	3.3	2.5	4.8	2.75	4.2	4.6

Do these data support the grower's claim at the 5% level of significance? (It can be assumed that the yield per plant is normally distributed).

This is a one tailed test since it is assumed that no one would complain if the yield was greater than stated. The null and alternative hypotheses are therefore:

$$H_0: \mu = 4 \text{ kg} \quad H_1: \mu < 4 \text{ kg}$$

The critical value on 7 degrees of freedom at a significance level of 5% for a one tailed test is –1.895.

The mean and standard deviation of the yield from this sample is:

$$\bar{x} = 3.74; \quad S = 0.7919$$

The best estimate of the population standard deviation is

$$0.7919 \times \sqrt{\frac{8}{7}} \quad = 0.8466$$

and:
$$\text{STEM} = \frac{0.8466}{\sqrt{8}}$$

$$= 0.2993$$

The test statistic is therefore:
$$t = \frac{3.74 - 4}{0.2993}$$

$$= -0.869$$

Since –0.869 is *greater* than –1.895, you cannot reject H_0. You may find it easier to ignore the negative signs and just compare 0.869 with 1.895, in which case 0.869 is *less* than 1.89). Alternatively you could draw a diagram as shown in Figure 6, below.

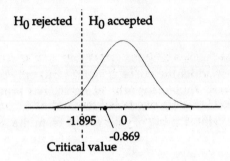

Figure 6

This diagram confirms that the test statistic is not in the critical region, and therefore it is not possible to reject H_0. That is, it hasn't been possible to disprove the grower's claim.

(Note: In practise the *experimental design* for this example would be a little more involved than has been suggested here)

7.6 The Chi squared hypothesis test

Is it possible to compare several percentages rather than just two? The short answer is yes, but a different kind of test has to be used. To use this new test you have to group the data into categories by *counting* the number of data items that have specific properties. The test statistic is then calculated using the following formula:

$$\sum \frac{(O - E)^2}{E}$$

Where 'O' represents the observed count and 'E' represents the expected count. The formula simply says 'find the difference between the observed and expected frequency of one category, square this value to remove any negative signs and then divide by the expected frequency for that category. Repeat this for all categories and sum the individual answers'.

This test statistic follows the χ^2 distribution (pronounced chi squared). The shape of this distribution depends on the degrees of freedom of the data. For example, for 4 degrees of freedom you would get the following shape.

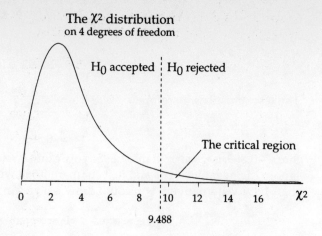

The χ^2 distribution
on 4 degrees of freedom

H_0 accepted H_0 rejected

The critical region

0   2   4   6   8   10   12   14   16 χ^2

9.488

Figure 7

The area under the curve is again 1 but only one tail is used for the critical region- the upper tail. The area representing 5% has been indicated and H_0 would be rejected if the test statistic was in this region.

The critical value of χ^2 is found from the χ^2 table that you will find in Appendix 2, page 137. For example, the critical value on 4 degrees of freedom at the 5% (0.05) significance level is 9.488.

Two applications of the χ^2 test will be illustrated here. The first is called the 'goodness of fit' test. The second is the 'contingency table' test or the 'test of association'.

7.6.1 The 'goodness of fit' test

Suppose you threw a six sided die 36 times. You would expect the faces numbered 1 to 6 to appear the same number of times, that is 6. However you might *observe* a rather different frequency.

Activity 6

Try this experiment for yourself and record the number of times each face appeared.

Suppose you got the following:

Face	1	2	3	4	5	6
Frequency	4	6	9	5	4	8

Is your observed frequency due to chance effects or does it indicate that the die is biased in any way? (in this example face 3 occurs most). The null hypothesis is that the die is fair and the alternate hypothesis is that it is biased, that is:

$$H_0: \text{Die is fair} \qquad H_1: \text{Die is biased}$$

Since the sum of the frequencies is fixed, you are 'free' to choose 5 of them; therefore the degrees of freedom is 5. From the χ^2 table, the critical value on 5 degrees of freedom and at the 5% significance level is 11.070. If the test statistic is greater than this value, H_0 will be rejected.

To calculate the χ^2 statistic you need to subtract the observed values from 6, square the result and then divide by 6. That is:

O	E	$(O-E)$	$(O-E)^2$	$\dfrac{(O-E)^2}{E}$
4	6	–2	4	0.667
6	6	0	0	0.000
9	6	3	9	1.500
5	6	–1	1	0.167
4	6	–2	4	0.667
8	6	2	4	0.667
				3.668

The sum of these values is 3.668 and this is compared with the critical value of 11.070. H_0 cannot be rejected and you would have to assume that the die was fair. The diagram below demonstrates that the test statistic is not in the critical region.

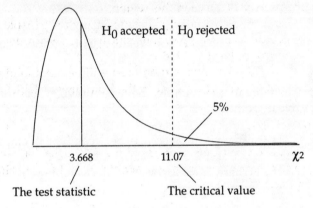

Figure 8

This is quite a simple application of the goodness of fit test since the expected values follow a uniform distribution (that is, each 'category' has the same expected value). However, the test can be applied to any situation where it is possible to calculate the expected values. The normal distribution (Chapter 5, page 74) is one example where these expected values could be calculated. In this example you might want to discover whether a set of data follows this distribution. The degrees of freedom are found from the formula:

$$v = n - 1 - k$$

Where 'n' is the number of pairs of observed and expected frequencies and 'k' is the number of population parameters estimated from the sample. For the normal distribution both the mean and the standard deviation have to be estimated, so k is 2 in this case.

7.6.2 The test of association

Example

The Personnel manager of a company believes that monthly paid staff take more time off work through sickness than those staff who are paid weekly (and do not belong to the company sickness scheme). To test this theory, the sickness records for 531 randomly selected employees who have been in continuous employment for the past year were analysed. The table shown below was produced, which placed employees into 3 categories according to how many days they were off work through sickness during the past year. For example, 95 monthly paid employees were off sick for less than 5 days.

Type of employee	*Number of days off sick*		
	Less than 5 days	*5 to 10 days*	*More than 10 days*
Monthly paid	95	47	18
Weekly paid	143	146	112

Activity 7

Is there any association between type of employee and numbers of days off sick?

The table in the example above is known as a *contingency* table. The null and alternative hypothesis are:

H_0: There is no *association* between type of employee and number of days off sick.

H_1: There is an association between type of employee and number of days off sick.

In order to calculate the χ^2 test statistic it is necessary to determine the expected values for each category. To do this you first have to work out the row and column totals as follows:

Type of employee	*Number of days off sick*			
	Less than 5 days	*5 to 10 days*	*More than 10 days*	*Total*
Monthly paid	95	47	18	160
Weekly paid	143	146	112	401
Total	238	193	130	561

You now need to apply some basic ideas of probability (see Chapter 4, page 54) to the problem.

If an employee was chosen at random, the probability that he was monthly paid would be $\frac{160}{561}$ and the probability that he would have been off sick for less than 5 days is $\frac{238}{561}$.

Therefore, using the multiplication rule for two probabilities, the probability that the person is both monthly paid and in the 'less than 5 days' category is $\frac{160}{561} \times \frac{238}{561}$.

Since there are 561 employees in total, the expected number of employees with both these attributes is

$$\frac{160}{561} \times \frac{238}{561} \times 561 = \frac{160 \times 238}{561} = 67.9$$

This could be written as:

$$\text{Expected value} = \frac{\text{Row total} \times \text{Column total}}{\text{Grand total}}$$

and is applicable for all cells of a contingency table. The rest of the expected values can now be worked out and a table set up similar to the one used for the 'goodness of fit' test (page 110).

O	E	$(O-E)$	$(O-E)^2$	$\frac{(O-E)^2}{E}$
95	67.9	27.1	734.41	10.816
47	55.0	−8.00	64.0	1.164
18	37.1	−19.1	364.81	9.833
143	170.1	−27.1	734.41	4.318
146	138.0	8.00	64.00	0.464
112	92.9	19.10	364.81	3.927
				30.522

The sum of the χ^2 values is 30.522 and this is the test statistic for this problem. The critical value depends on the degrees of freedom of this table. As you know, degrees of freedom relates to the number of values that you are free to choose. If, for example, you choose the value for the top left hand cell, the bottom left hand cell is determined since the two cells must add to 238. Likewise you could choose the next cell along, but then all other cells are determined for you. So, for this problem, there are 2 degrees of freedom. Fortunately, there is a formula for calculating the degrees of freedom and is:

$$(\text{number of columns} - 1) \times (\text{number of rows} - 1)$$

In the table above, there are 3 columns (excluding the total column) and 2 rows, so the degrees of freedom are:

$$(3 - 1) \times (2 - 1) = 2$$

The critical value for 2 degrees of freedom at the 5% significance level is 5.991 and at the 0.1% significance level it is 13.816. Therefore, since the test statistic is greater than 13.816, H_0 can be rejected at the 0.1% significance level and you could conclude that there does seem to be an association between staff category and the number of days off sick.

It is possible to be more specific about this association by looking at the individual χ^2 values and also the (O − E) column. The two largest values χ^2 values are 10.816 and 9.883. These both relate to the monthly paid staff and it suggests that this group of employees have a higher frequency in the 'less than 5 days category' than expected but a lower frequency in the 'more than 10 days' category.

The χ^2 test for association is a very important and useful test in the area of statistics in particular and decision making in general. However there are a few problems that you need to be aware of.

Low expected values

The test statistic follows the χ^2 distribution provided the expected values are not too small. The guideline that is normally adopted is that the expected value for any cell should be greater than 5. If an expected value less than 5 occurs it is possible to combine categories until this value is achieved. Of course there must be at least 3 rows or 3 columns to be able to do this.

Two by two tables

The χ^2 distribution is a continuous distribution, whereas the sample data is discrete. Normally the sample size is sufficient to avoid making a continuity correction, but this will be needed for 2×2 tables. The correction required is to subtract 0.5 from the *absolute* value of the difference between the observed and expected values. For example, if the difference was –2.7, the corrected value would be –2.2 (not –3.2)

Tables of percentages

The χ^2 test is applied to tables of frequencies not percentages. If you are given a table of percentages you will need to convert it to frequencies by multiplying each percentage by the total frequency. If you are not given the total frequency then it is not possible to use this test.

7.7 Summary

This chapter has introduced you to a few important tests that can be carried out on sample data. These tests are called hypothesis tests because some hypothesis is made concerning a population parameter. A test is then applied to the sample data and the hypothesis can either be accepted or rejected. If the hypothesis is rejected then an alternative hypothesis is accepted. For the test of a percentage the sample size has to be large and the percentage to be tested should not be extreme. If these conditions are met the Z-test can be applied to the sample data. The Z-test can also be applied to a population mean provided the standard deviation of the population is known or the sample size is large. If neither of these conditions can be met then the t-test should be used. The other test you were introduced to was the χ^2 (Chi squared) test. This test can be applied to a frequency distribution to see if the distribution follows some known one or it can be applied to see if there is an association between categories.

7.8 Further reading

Morris, C, *Quantitative Approaches in Business Studies*, Pitman, 1993, Chapter 11

Oakshott, L, *Quantitative Approaches to Decision Making*, DP Publications, 1993, Unit 8.

Lucey, T, *Quantitative Techniques*, DP Publications, 1992, Chapter 6.

7.9 Exercises

Progress questions

These question have been designed to help you remember the key points in this chapter. The answers to these questions are given in Appendix 1, page 134.

Give the missing word in each case.

1. H_0 is called the .... hypothesis.

2. H_1 is called the .... hypothesis.

3. The boundaries of the critical region are called .... values.

4. The test using the normal distribution is called the ...... test.

5. For a two tailed test at 5% confidence interval, the area in each tail is ....

6. The chi test is applied to .... data.

Answer TRUE or FALSE

7. If the critical value is 1.96 and the test statistic is 2.34 the null hypothesis should be rejected.

    True ☐ False ☐

8. In order to decide whether to use a one or two tailed test you would inspect the data.

    True ☐ False ☐

9. You would use the t-test if the population cannot be assumed to be normal

    True ☐ False ☐

10. Only one tail of the distribution is used in the Chi squared test.

    True ☐ False ☐

11. The Chi squared distribution is symmetrical about the mean.

    True ☐ False ☐

12. The Chi squared test cannot be applied to a table of percentages.

    True ☐ False ☐

13. The sample percentage P is used to calculate STEP when carrying out a hypothesis test of a percentage.

    True ☐ False ☐

Review questions

These questions have been designed to help you check your comprehension of the key points in this chapter. You may wish to look further than this chapter in order to answer them fully. You will find the reading list useful in this respect. You can check the essential elements of your answers by referring to the appropriate section.

14. Under what circumstances would you use a one tailed test rather than a two tailed one? (Section 7.3)

15. Why is it preferable to use large samples for hypothesis tests? (Sections 7.3 and 7.4)

16. What is the difference between a Z test and a t test for a sample mean? (Sections 7.3 and 7.5)

17. What problems might you come across in carrying out the chi square test and how would you overcome them? (Section 7.6)

Multiple choice questions

The answers to these will be given in the Lecturers' Supplement.

18. The null hypothesis for a one tailed test can be of the form:
    A $\mu =$
    B $\mu \neq$
    C $\mu <$ or $\mu >$

19. The degrees of freedom for a t-test of a mean if the sample size is 10 is:
    A 10
    B 9
    C 11

20. The degrees of freedom for a contingency table of size 2 by 5 is:
    A 10
    B 7
    C 4
    D 3

21. Expected values in a contingency table should be:
    A greater than 5
    B less than 5
    C greater than 30

22. The critical region is in:
    A The tails of a distribution
    B The middle of a distribution
    C Either the middle or the tails of a distribution.

23. The chi square distribution is:
    A Symmetrical about a mean value
    B Right skewed
    C Left skewed

24. If a significance level of 1% is used rather than 5% the null hypothesis is:
    A More likely to be rejected
    B Less likely to be rejected
    C Just as likely to be rejected

Practice questions

Answers to these questions will be given in the Lecturers' Supplement.

25. What is the critical value for a two sided Z-test at 5% significance?

26. What is the critical t value at 1% significance for a sample size of 12?

27. What is the critical Chi squared value for a contingency table of size 4×3 at 5% significance?

28. A company has analysed the time its customers take to pay an invoice over the past few years and has found that the distribution is normal with mean of 5.8 weeks and a standard deviation of 2.3 weeks. In order to speed up payment the company threatened to charge interest if bills were not paid within 3 weeks. A sample of 10 customers was then analysed and the mean time to pay had been reduced to 4.9 weeks. Is there any evidence that the mean time for all its customers has actually been reduced?

29. A motorcycle is claimed to have a fuel consumption which is normally distributed with mean 54 miles per gallon and a standard deviation of 5 miles per gallon. 12 motorcycles are tested and the mean value of their fuel consumption was found to be 50.5 miles per gallon.

    Taking a 5% level of significance test the hypothesis that the mean fuel consumption is 54 miles per gallon.

30. The lifetime of electric lightbulbs produced by a given process is normally distributed and is claimed to have a mean lifetime of 1500 hours. A batch of 50 was taken, which showed a mean lifetime of 1410 hours. The standard deviation of the sample is 90 hours. Test the hypothesis that the mean lifetime of the electric lightbulbs has not changed.

31. A company has been accused of selling underweight products. This product is supposed to weigh 500g and a sample of 6 was weighed and the results were:

    $$495, 512, 480, 505, 490, 502$$

    Is there any evidence that the mean weight is less than 500g?

32. The Speedwell Building Society has claimed that there has been a significant increase in the percentage of its customers taking out fixed rate mortgages. In the past, 30% of customers had this type of mortgage but during the past week 60 out of 150 new mortgages have been at a fixed rate. Is the claim by the building society correct?

33. The number of accidents occurring at a large construction site during the past week has been as follows:

Mon	Tue	Wed	Thurs	Fri
6	5	6	8	12

    Is there any evidence that accidents are more likely on certain days of the week?

34. In Britain a survey was carried out on 200 radio listeners who were asked what radio station they listened to most during an average week. A summary of their replies is given in the following table, together with their age range.

	Age range		
	less than 20	20 to 30	over 30
BBC	22	16	50
Local radio	6	11	16
Commercial	35	3	12

a) Is there any evidence that there is an association between age and radio station?

b) By considering the contribution to the value of your test statistic from each cell and the relative sizes of the observed and expected frequencies in each cell, indicate the main source of the association, if any exists.

Assignment

Answers to this assignment are included in the Lecturers' Supplement.

In order to assess the effectiveness of a company training programme, each employee was appraised before and after the training. Based on the comparisons of the two appraisals each of the 110 production staff were classified according to how well they had benefited from the training. This classification ranged from 'worse', which means they now perform worse than they did before, to 'high', which means they perform much better than they did before the training. The results of this appraisal can be seen in the table below where you will notice that employees have been further classified by age.

Age of employee	Level of improvement				
	Worse	None	Some	High	Total
Below 40	1	5	24	30	60
40+	4	5	31	10	50
Total	5	10	55	40	110

a) Is there any association between level of improvement at the job and age?

b) What is the 95% confidence interval for the percentage of employees who showed a high level of improvement at their job.

8 *Correlation and regression*

8.1 *Introduction*

The statistical analysis that you have covered so far has been concerned with the characteristics of a single variable. However, it also might be of interest to look at two variables simultaneously. For instance you might suspect that the cost of production is dependent on the quantity produced or that sales of a product are related to price. This chapter introduces two techniques; correlation to measure the association between two variables and regression to obtain the relationship between the variables.

On completing this chapter, you should be able to:

❏ Draw and interpret scatter diagrams

❏ Calculate Spearman's rank correlation coefficient

❏ Calculate Pearson's product moment correlation Coefficient

❏ Obtain and use the least squares regression line

❏ Appreciate the limitations of the techniques

8.2 *Scatter diagrams*

A scatter diagram is simply a way of representing a set of bivariate data by a scatter of plots. One variable is plotted on the X axis and the other on the Y axis. Normally the 'X' variable (the *independent* variable) is the one that you believe influences the 'Y' variable (the *dependent* variable). That is Y *depends* on X.

Examples of scatter diagrams are given in Figure 1 below. The first diagram indicates a *positive correlation* because as the number of deliveries increases so apparently does the delivery time. The second diagram indicates a *negative correlation* because as the air temperature increases the heating cost falls. The third diagram suggests that no correlation exists between salary and age of employees. The fourth diagram suggests that the quantity produced and the efficiency of a machine are correlated but not linearly.

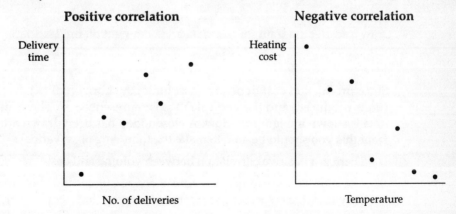

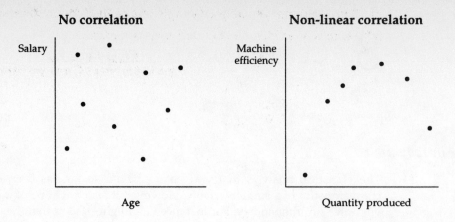

Figure 1 Examples of scatter diagrams

When categorising scatter diagrams you may find it easier to draw a closed loop around the points. This loop should be drawn so that it encloses all the points but at the same time making the area within the loop as small as possible. If the loop looks like a circle, this suggests that there is little, if any, correlation, but if the loop looks more like an ellipse then this suggests that there is some correlation present. An ellipse pointing upwards would represent a positive correlation and one pointing downwards would represent a negative correlation. If you try this with diagrams 1 to 3 above you will see that this agrees with the statements already made. A loop around the points in diagram 4 would clearly show the non-linear nature of the association.

The closer the ellipse becomes to a straight line, the stronger the correlation. If the ellipse became a straight line you would say that you have perfect correlation. (Unless the straight line was horizontal, in which case there can be no correlation since the dependent variable has a constant value).

Example 1

The production manager at Lookwools Engineering suspects that there is an association between production volume and production cost. To prove this he obtained the total cost of production for different production volumes and the data is as follows:

Units produced (000's)	1	2	3	4	5	6
Production costs(£000's)	5.0	10.5	15.5	25.0	16.0	22.5

Activity 1

Draw a scatter diagram for this data and comment on the association (if any).

Since production cost depends on volume, the horizontal (X) axis represents volume (units produced) and the vertical (Y) axis represents cost. The scatter diagram for this data is shown in Figure 2 below. A closed loop has been drawn around the points and from this you should be able to make the following observations:

i)   There is a positive correlation between volume and cost.

ii) The loop is a fairly narrow ellipse shape suggesting that, for the range of data provided, the association is reasonably strong (but not perfect).

iii) If the point representing 4000 units was omitted the ellipse would be narrower.

iv) There is no evidence of non-linearity in the data.

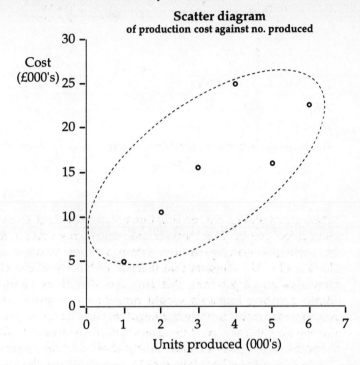

Figure 2

Although these observations are valid the sample size is rather small to make definite conclusions. In practise a larger sample size would be advisable (at least twelve pairs) and the cost of 4000 units would be checked. Sometimes these 'rogue' results suggest that other factors are influencing the dependent variable and further investigation is necessary.

8.3 *Measures of correlation*

The technique of correlation measures the strength of the association between the variables. There are two widely used measures of correlation. These are Spearman's rank correlation coefficient and Pearson's product moment correlation coefficient. Both give a value between −1 and 1 so that −1 indicates a perfect negative correlation, +1 a perfect positive correlation and zero indicates no correlation. This is illustrated in Figure 3 below.

Range of values of the correlation coefficient

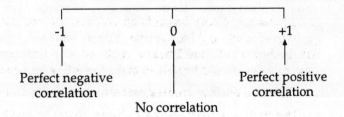

Figure 3

8.3.1   Spearman's rank correlation coefficient (R)

This method involves ranking each value of X and Y and using the following formula to calculate the coefficient 'R'.

$$R = 1 - \frac{6\sum d^2}{n(n^2 - 1)}$$

Where d is the difference in rank between pairs and n is the number of pairs. The value of R lies between +1 and −1.

The procedure to calculate this coefficient is as follows:

1. Rank both variables so that either the largest is ranked 1 or alternatively the smallest is ranked 1.

2. For each pair obtain the difference between the rankings.

3. Square these differences and sum.

4. Substitute the sum of these differences into the formula

If during step 1 you find you have equal rankings for the same variable it is the *mean* of the rankings that is used. For example, if rank 3 occurs twice then both should be given a ranking of 3.5. The next ranking is 5.

Activity 2

Calculate Spearman's rank correlation coefficient for the data given in Example 1.

Step 1   Rank both variables

If you use rank 1 as being the lowest and rank 6 as the largest value then the 'Units Produced' are already ranked for you. 'Production Costs' start at 5.0 (£000's) and this will have a rank 1, while 25.0 is the largest and will be given a rank of 6. This can be seen in the table below.

Units produced (000's)	1	2	3	4	5	6
Rank	1	2	3	4	5	6
Production costs(£000's)	5.0	10.5	15.5	25.0	16.0	22.5
Rank	1	2	3	6	4	5

Steps 2 and 3   Calculate differences, square and sum

You will find it easier if you set out the calculations in a table similar to the one below:

No of units	Cost	Difference (d)	d^2
1	1	0	0
2	2	0	0
3	3	0	0
4	6	–2	4
5	4	1	1
6	5	1	1
		Sum	6

Step 4   Substitute the sum of d^2 into the formula

The sum of d^2 is 6 and there are 6 pairs of values so Spearman's rank correlation coefficient is:

$$R = 1 - \frac{6 \times 6}{6(6^2 - 1)}$$

$$= 1 - \frac{36}{6 \times 35}$$

$$= 0.829$$

This value is close to +1 which supports the assessment made from the scatter diagram that there is a fairly strong positive association between cost of production and production volume.

Data does not always consist of actual measurements. For example, in market research, data may consist of opinions on a particular product. This kind of data is called ordinal data. Ordinal data has the property that although they do not have actual numerical values, they can be ranked.

The next example should help you understand how to apply Spearman's method to ordinal data.

Example 2

BSL marketing have been asked to conduct a survey into the publics attitude to a new chocolate bar. A pilot survey was carried out by asking 5 people of different ages to try the product and give their reaction. The result of this survey is as follows:

Person	Age range	Response
A	below 10	very good
B	15 to 20	fair
C	20 to 25	fair
D	10 to 15	excellent
E	over 25	disliked

Activity 3

Is there any evidence of an association between age and preference for the product?

Both the age range and response can be ranked. It doesn't really matter how you rank them as long as you take your method into account when you come to interpret your coefficient. In the calculations that follow I have used low rankings for low age range and low rankings for the low response ratings (that is, 'disliked' has a ranking of 1). Using this method the rankings are as follows:

Person	Age range	Rank	Response	Rank
A	below 10	1	very good	4
B	15 to 20	3	fair	2
C	20 to 25	4	fair	2
D	10 to 15	2	excellent	5
E	over 25	5	disliked	1

Notice that both B and C are ranked equal second in their responses. To compensate for the missing third rank a *mean* rank of 2.5 is used instead of rank 2. You can see this in the following table.

Person	Age range	Response	Difference(d)	d^2
A	1	4	−3	9.00
B	3	2.5	0.5	0.25
C	4	2.5	1.5	2.25
D	2	5	−3	9.00
E	5	1	4	16.00
			Sum	36.50

The sum of the square of the differences is 36.5 and substituting this value into the formula gives:

$$R = 1 - \frac{6 \times 36.5}{5 \times (5^2 - 1)}$$

$$= 1 - \frac{219}{120}$$

$$= -0.825$$

This value is fairly large, which suggests an association between age and response. Since the coefficient is negative, it would appear that younger people are more likely to react favourably to the product.

8.3.2 Pearson's product moment correlation coefficient (r)

This measure of correlation tends to be the most popular but it can only be used when the data is on the interval scale of measurement. That is the data consists of actual measurements. The formula for r is:

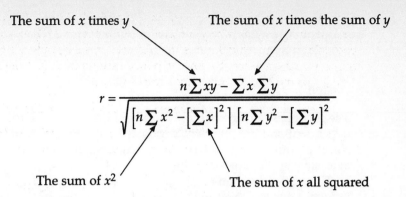

The sum of x times y — The sum of x times the sum of y

$$r = \frac{n \sum xy - \sum x \sum y}{\sqrt{\left[n \sum x^2 - \left[\sum x \right]^2 \right] \left[n \sum y^2 - \left[\sum y \right]^2 \right]}}$$

The sum of x^2 — The sum of x all squared

This formula looks daunting at first sight but it is quite straightforward to use as you will see by attempting Activity 4.

Activity 4

Calculate the Pearson's product moment correlation coefficient for the data given in Example 1.

To obtain this coefficient you are advised to set out the calculations in tabular form, as follows:

Units produced	Production cost			
x	y	xy	x^2	y^2
1	5.0	5.0	1	25.0
2	10.5	21.0	4	110.25
3	15.5	46.5	9	240.25
4	25.0	100.0	16	625.00
5	16.0	80.0	25	256.00
6	22.5	135.0	36	506.25
$\sum x = 21$	$\sum y = 94.5$	$\sum xy = 387.5$	$\sum x^2 = 91$	$\sum y^2 = 1762.75$

The summations can then be substituted into the formula for **r**:

$$\mathbf{r} = \frac{6 \times 387.5 - 21 \times 94.5}{\sqrt{\left(6 \times 91 - (21)^2 \right)\left(6 \times 1762.75 - (94.5)^2 \right)}}$$

$$= \frac{340.5}{\sqrt{105 \times 1646.25}}$$

$$= \frac{340.5}{415.7599}$$

$$= 0.8190$$

This calculation agrees with Spearman's calculation (see Activity 2) in that there is a strong positive correlation between production volume and cost.

Pearson's product moment correlation coefficient is a more accurate measure of the correlation between two *numeric* variables. However, it cannot be applied to non-numeric data.

8.4 Linear regression

The technique of linear regression attempts to define the relationship between the dependent and independent variables by the means of a linear equation. This is the simplest form of equation between two variables and fortunately many situations can at least be approximated by this type of relationship.

The scatter diagram for the production cost data of Example 1 has been reproduced in Figure 4 below. You will see that a line has been drawn through the data and this line represents the linear relationship between the two variables. However, since the relationship is not perfect it is possible to draw several different lines 'by eye' through the diagram, each of which would look reasonable. However each line would represent a slightly different relationship as the gradient and/or intercept on the Y axis would be different. To decide how good a particular line is, you could find the difference between each point and the line. These differences are often referred to as the 'errors' between the actual value and that predicted by the line.

These errors have been represented by vertical lines on the diagram. Note that the errors below the line are negative and those above the line are positive. If you add these errors you will find that the total error is about zero. Does this prove that the line is a good one? Unfortunately not, because the zero value is only obtained by adding positive and negative values. Many more lines could be found that also would give a total error of zero. The errors could be added, ignoring the sign but it can be shown that the best line or the *'line of best fit'* is obtained when the sum of the squares of the errors is minimised. Squaring the errors not only removes the minus sign but it also gives more emphasis to the large errors.

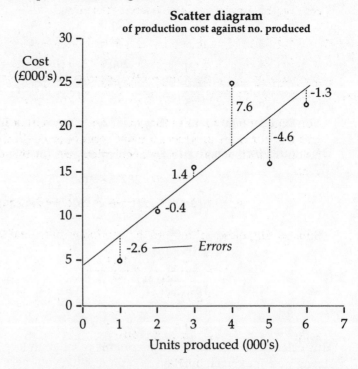

Figure 4

8.5 The method of least squares

Linear regression involves finding that line that minimises the sum of squares of the errors. The theory behind 'the method of least squares' is beyond the scope of this book but the application of the theory is straightforward. The most important part is to ensure that the Y variable is the dependent variable-so, for example, the production cost depends on the number of units produced.

The linear regression model is given in the form:

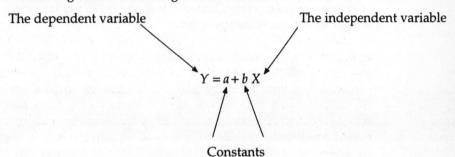

The dependent variable   The independent variable

$$Y = a + b\,X$$

Constants

The values of '**a**' and '**b**' that minimise the squared errors are given by the equations:-

$$b = \frac{n\sum xy - \sum x \sum y}{n\sum x^2 - \left(\sum x\right)^2}$$

$$a = \frac{\sum y}{n} - b\frac{\sum x}{n}$$

You can think of '*b*' as the slope of the regression line and '*a*' as the value of the intercept on the Y axis (value of Y when X is zero).

Activity 5

Calculate the regression line for the production cost data given in Example 1.

You will probably realise that there are many similarities between the formula for b and that for r, the product moment correlation coefficient (page 125). Since the correlation coefficient has already been calculated for this data (Activity 4) you can note that:

$$\Sigma x = 21,\ \Sigma y = 94.5,\ \Sigma xy = 387.5 \text{ and } \Sigma x^2 = 91$$

Substituting these values into the equations for '**a**' and '**b**' give:

$$b = \frac{6 \times 387.5 - 21 \times 94.5}{6 \times 91 - 21^2}$$
$$= 3.2429$$

and:
$$a = \frac{94.5}{6} - 3.2429 \times \frac{21}{6}$$
$$= 4.3999$$

The regression equation for this data is therefore:

$$Y = 4.4 + 3.24X$$

This suggests that for every 1 unit (1000) rise in production volume, the production cost would rise by, on average 3.24 units (£3,240) and that when nothing is produced ($X = 0$), the production cost would still be £4400. This probably can be explained by factory overhead costs that are incurred even when there is no production.

In order to estimate the value of Y for a particular value of X, this X value is substituted into the above equation.

Activity 6

Calculate the cost of production for production volumes of

a) 2500 units and   b) 20,000 units

Have you any reservations regarding the costs obtained?

To obtain the cost of production for these two cases you would simply substitute the values of 2.5 and 20 into the above equation. That is:

a) $Y = 4.4 + 3.24 \times 2.5$

               $= 12.5$

So 2500 units would cost about £12,500 on average.

b) $Y = 4.4 + 3.24 \times 20$

               $= 69.2$

and 20,000 units would cost £69,200 on average. However, 20,000 units is well *outside* the range of data used in the original analysis. You cannot be certain that the relationship between cost and volume will remain linear outside this range and so it would be unwise placing too much reliance on the predicted figure.

8.6 Coefficient of Determination

Before a regression equation can be used effectively as a predictor for the dependent variable, it is necessary to decide how well it fits the data. One statistic that gives this information is the Coefficient of Determination. This measures the proportion of the variation in the dependent variable explained by the variation in the independent variable. It is given by r^2, which is the square of the product moment correlation coefficient.

Activity 7

What is the value of r^2 for the production cost data of Example 1?

The value of r is 0.8190 so $r^2 = 0.671$ which means that 0.67 or 67% of the variation in production cost is explained by the production volume. Alternatively, 33% of the variation is not explained.

8.7 Summary

The techniques introduced in this chapter have enabled you to obtain answers to the following questions.

i) Is there an association between the variables?

ii) How strong is this association?

iii) What is the relationship between the variables?

You used scatter diagrams to look at the association between the variables, while correlation enabled you to quantify this association. Linear regression was used to describe the nature of the relationship between the variables.

8.8 Further reading

Morris, C, *Quantitative Approaches in Business Studies*, Pitman, 1993, Chapters 12 and 13.

Harper, W, *Statistics, M & E Handbook Series*, Pitman, 1991, Chapters 12, 13 and 14.

Oakshott, L, *Quantitative Approaches to Decision Making*, DP Publications, 1993, Units 12 and 13.

Lucey, T, *Quantitative Techniques*, DP Publications, 1992, Chapter 7.

8.9 Exercises

Progress questions

These question have been designed to help you remember the key points in this chapter. The answers to these questions are given in Appendix 1, page 134.

Give the missing word in each case:

1. A graphical picture of bivariate data is called a .... diagram.

2. Correlation measures the strength of the............ between two variables.

3. Regression defines the .... between the two variables.

4. Correlation is measured on a scale from ...... to ....

5. The least squares regression line .... the sum of the squared errors.

6. A perfect relationship between two variables means that all the points lie on a .... line.

7. Spearman's rank correlation coefficient is used for .... data.

Answer TRUE or FALSE

8. A high correlation confirms a causal relationship.

    True ☐ False ☐

9. A negative correlation coefficient means that there is no association between the two variables.

    True ☐ False ☐

10. Pearson's product moment correlation coefficient can only be calculated for numerical data.

True ☐ False ☐

11. The coefficient 'b' in the linear regression model represents the slope of the regression line.

True ☐ False ☐

Review questions

These questions have been designed to help you check your comprehension of the key points in this chapter. You may wish to look further than this chapter in order to answer them fully. You will find the reading list useful in this respect. You can check the essential elements of your answers by referring to the appropriate section.

12. What is a scatter diagram and why is it important to draw this diagram before any calculations are carried out? (Section 8.2)

13. What are the essential differences between Spearman's rank correlation coefficient and Pearson's product moment correlation coefficient? (Section 8.3)

14. What do you understand by the expression 'method of least squares'? (Section 8.5)

Multiple choice questions

The answers to these will be given in the Lecturers' Supplement.

15. If the increase in one variable causes an increase in the another variable, the form of the correlation between the variables must be:
    A   positive
    B   negative
    C   perfect

16. The dependent variable is plotted on the:
    A   X axis
    B   Y axis
    C   either axis

17. If the value of r is 0.8 then the coefficient of determination is:
    A   0.8
    B   0.64
    C   80

18. If pairs of bivariate data all have equal rank then Spearman's rank correlation coefficient must be:
    A   0
    B   +1
    C   −1

19. If Spearman's rank correlation coefficient is −1 for a set of numerate bivariate data then Pearson's product moment correlation coefficient for the same data must be:
    A   +1
    B   −1
    C   0
    D   between 0 and +1
    E   between 0 and −1

20. If the coefficient 'b' in the linear regression model is zero then the correlation between the two variables must be:

    A   +1

    B   −1

    C   0

Practice questions

Answers to these questions will be given in the Lecturers' Supplement.

21. A regression line is Y = 3 + 5X. What is the value of Y if X = 2.

22. The data below relates to the weight and height of a group of students.

Height (ins)	Weight (lbs)	Sex
68	148	male
69	126	female
66	145	male
70	158	male
66	140	female
68	126	female
64	120	female
66	119	female
70	182	male
62	127	female
68	165	male
63	133	male
65	124	female
73	203	male

a) Draw a scatter diagram of weight against height for the whole data. Alongside each point write either 'm' or 'f' as appropriate.

b) Describe your scatter diagram. Try drawing an ellipse around

    i)   all the points

    ii) the points relating to the male students

    iii) the points relating to the female students.

    Is there any indication that the correlation is stronger for either group?

c) Calculate Person's Product Moment Correlation Coefficient for the three sets of points identified in (b) above. Comment on the values obtained.

(Collect data from a group of friends and repeat the analysis)

23. A group of students compared the results they obtained in a quantitative methods assignment and a law assignment. The results by position in a group of 50 was as follows:

Student	A	B	C	D	E	F	G	H	I
Quants	5	8	45	2	9	5	15	20	3
Law	29	17	1	11	6	18	33	3	8

Use Spearman's rank correlation coefficient to discover if there is any correlation between position in each subject

24. A company is investigating the relationship between sales and advertising revenue. Data has been collected on these two variables and is shown below: (All figures are in £000's).

Mth	Jan	Feb	Mar	Apr	May	June	Jul	Aug	Sept	Oct	Nov	Dec
Sales	60	60	58	45	41	33	31	25	24	23	23	23
Adv.	6.0	6.0	6.0	5.8	4.5	4.1	3.3	3.1	2.5	2.4	2.3	2.3

a) Plot a scatter diagram of the data given in the table above. Comment on the strength of the association between the two variables.

b) Obtain the least squares regression line and comment on how well it fits the data.

c) What would the expected sales be given an advertising expenditure of £5000.

Assignment

Answers to this assignment are included in the Lecturers' Supplement.

It seems reasonable to assume that the second hand price of a particular make of car is dependent on its age. Decide on a particular make and model of car and a suitable source for the data, such as your local newspaper. Collect data on the age and price of around 20 cars and do the following:

a) Plot a scatter graph of the data. Does the scatter graph indicate that a linear relationship exists for all or part of the range of the data?

b) Calculate the regression equation that would enable the price of the car to be obtained given its age.

c) Using the equation obtained in (ii) above and suitable examples, illustrate how the price of a car could be found if its age was known. Within what age range is your equation valid? Why is this so?

d) What proportion of the variability in price is explained by the age factor? What other factors could affect the price of a car?

Appendices

Appendix 1 Answers to Progress questions

Chapter 1 Survey Methods

1. Target	2. Sample	3. Frame	4. Random
5. Bias	6. Error	7. Stratified	8. Systematic
9. True	10. False	11. True	12. False
13. True			

Chapter 2 Presentation of Data

1. Primary	2. Discrete	3. Continuous	4. Tally
5. Pie	6. Component	7. Grouped	8. Polygon
9. True	10. False	11. True	12. False
13. True	14. True		

Chapter 3 Summarising Data

1. Sum	2. Middle	3. Frequently	4. Range
5. 50	6. Deviation	7. Standard deviation	
8. Shape	9. False	10. True	11. True
12. False	13. True	14. False	

Chapter 4 Probability and Decision-Making

1. 1 or 100%	2. Empirical	3. Subjective	4. 1
5. Addition	6. Multiplication	7. Expected	8. Trees
9. True	10. False	11. True	12. True
13. True	14. False		

Chapter 5 The Normal Distribution

1. Symmetrical	2. 1 or 100%	3. Mean and Standard deviation
4. Increases	5. Continuous	6. False	7. True
8. True	9. False		

Chapter 6 Analysis and Interpretation of Sample Data

1. Population	2. Sample	3. Point	4. Sample
5. Less	6. Confidence	7. False	8. True
9. False	10. True	11. False	12. True
13. True	14. False		

Chapter 7 Testing a Hypothesis

1. Null	2. Alternative	3. Critical	4. Z
5. 2.5%	6. Categorical	7. True	8. False
9. False	10. True	11. False	12. True
13. False			

Chapter 8 Correlation and Regression

1. Scatter	2. Association	3. Relationship	4. -1, +1
5. Minimises	6. Straight	7. Ordinal	8. False
9. False	10. True	11. True	

Appendix 2 Statistical tables

Areas in the right hand tail of the standard normal distribution

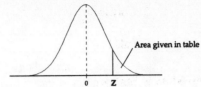

Area given in table

Z	0.00	0.01	0.02	0.03	0.04	0.05	0.06	0.07	0.08	0.09
0.0	0.5000	0.4960	0.4920	0.4880	0.4840	0.4801	0.4761	0.4721	0.4681	0.4641
0.1	0.4602	0.4562	0.4522	0.4483	0.4443	0.4404	0.4364	0.4325	0.4286	0.4247
0.2	0.4207	0.4168	0.4129	0.4090	0.4052	0.4013	0.3974	0.3936	0.3897	0.3859
0.3	0.3821	0.3783	0.3745	0.3707	0.3669	0.3632	0.3594	0.3557	0.3520	0.3483
0.4	0.3446	0.3409	0.3372	0.3336	0.3300	0.3264	0.3228	0.3192	0.3156	0.3121
0.5	0.3085	0.3050	0.3015	0.2981	0.2946	0.2912	0.2877	0.2843	0.2810	0.2776
0.6	0.2743	0.2709	0.2676	0.2643	0.2611	0.2578	0.2546	0.2514	0.2483	0.2451
0.7	0.2420	0.2389	0.2358	0.2327	0.2296	0.2266	0.2236	0.2206	0.2177	0.2148
0.8	0.2119	0.2090	0.2061	0.2033	0.2005	0.1977	0.1949	0.1922	0.1894	0.1867
0.9	0.1841	0.1814	0.1788	0.1762	0.1736	0.1711	0.1685	0.1660	0.1635	0.1611
1.0	0.1587	0.1562	0.1539	0.1515	0.1492	0.1469	0.1446	0.1423	0.1401	0.1379
1.1	0.1357	0.1335	0.1314	0.1292	0.1271	0.1251	0.1230	0.1210	0.1190	0.1170
1.2	0.1151	0.1131	0.1112	0.1093	0.1075	0.1056	0.1038	0.1020	0.1003	0.0985
1.3	0.0968	0.0951	0.0934	0.0918	0.0901	0.0885	0.0869	0.0853	0.0838	0.0823
1.4	0.0808	0.0793	0.0778	0.0764	0.0749	0.0735	0.0721	0.0708	0.0694	0.0681
1.5	0.0668	0.0655	0.0643	0.0630	0.0618	0.0606	0.0594	0.0582	0.0571	0.0559
1.6	0.0548	0.0537	0.0526	0.0516	0.0505	0.0495	0.0485	0.0475	0.0465	0.0455
1.7	0.0446	0.0436	0.0427	0.0418	0.0409	0.0401	0.0392	0.0384	0.0375	0.0367
1.8	0.0359	0.0351	0.0344	0.0336	0.0329	0.0322	0.0314	0.0307	0.0301	0.0294
1.9	0.0287	0.0281	0.0274	0.0268	0.0262	0.0256	0.0250	0.0244	0.0239	0.0233
2.0	0.0228	0.0222	0.0217	0.0212	0.0207	0.0202	0.0197	0.0192	0.0188	0.0183
2.1	0.0179	0.0174	0.0170	0.0166	0.0162	0.0158	0.0154	0.0150	0.0146	0.0143
2.2	0.0139	0.0136	0.0132	0.0129	0.0125	0.0122	0.0119	0.0116	0.0113	0.0110
2.3	0.0107	0.0104	0.0102	0.0099	0.0096	0.0094	0.0091	0.0089	0.0087	0.0084
2.4	0.0082	0.0080	0.0078	0.0075	0.0073	0.0071	0.0069	0.0068	0.0066	0.0064
2.5	0.0062	0.0060	0.0059	0.0057	0.0055	0.0054	0.0052	0.0051	0.0049	0.0048
2.6	0.0047	0.0045	0.0044	0.0043	0.0041	0.0040	0.0039	0.0038	0.0037	0.0036
2.7	0.0035	0.0034	0.0033	0.0032	0.0031	0.0030	0.0029	0.0028	0.0027	0.0026
2.8	0.0026	0.0025	0.0024	0.0023	0.0023	0.0022	0.0021	0.0021	0.0020	0.0019
2.9	0.0019	0.0018	0.0018	0.0017	0.0016	0.0016	0.0015	0.0015	0.0014	0.0014

3.0 0.0013   3.1 0.0010   3.2 0.0007   3.3 0.0005   3.4 0.0003

Table of the t-distribution

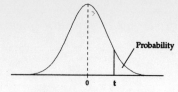

Probability

df	0.2	0.1	0.05	0.025	0.01	0.005	0.001	0.0001
1	1.376	3.078	6.314	12.706	31.821	63.657	318.309	3183.1
2	1.061	1.886	2.920	4.303	6.965	9.925	22.327	70.700
3	0.978	1.638	2.353	3.182	4.541	5.841	10.215	22.204
4	0.941	1.533	2.132	2.776	3.747	4.604	7.173	13.034
5	0.920	1.476	2.015	2.571	3.365	4.032	5.893	9.678
6	0.906	1.440	1.943	2.447	3.143	3.707	5.208	8.025
7	0.896	1.415	1.895	2.365	2.998	3.499	4.785	7.063
8	0.889	1.397	1.860	2.306	2.896	3.355	4.501	6.442
9	0.883	1.383	1.833	2.262	2.821	3.250	4.297	6.010
10	0.879	1.372	1.812	2.228	2.764	3.169	4.144	5.694
11	0.876	1.363	1.796	2.201	2.718	3.106	4.025	5.453
12	0.873	1.356	1.782	2.179	2.681	3.055	3.930	5.263
13	0.870	1.350	1.771	2.160	2.650	3.012	3.852	5.111
14	0.868	1.345	1.761	2.145	2.624	2.977	3.787	4.985
15	0.866	1.341	1.753	2.131	2.602	2.947	3.733	4.880
16	0.865	1.337	1.746	2.120	2.583	2.921	3.686	4.791
17	0.863	1.333	1.740	2.110	2.567	2.898	3.646	4.714
18	0.862	1.330	1.734	2.101	2.552	2.878	3.610	4.648
19	0.861	1.328	1.729	2.093	2.539	2.861	3.579	4.590
20	0.860	1.325	1.725	2.086	2.528	2.845	3.552	4.539
21	0.859	1.323	1.721	2.080	2.518	2.831	3.527	4.493
22	0.858	1.321	1.717	2.074	2.508	2.819	3.505	4.452
23	0.858	1.319	1.714	2.069	2.500	2.807	3.485	4.415
24	0.857	1.318	1.711	2.064	2.492	2.797	3.467	4.382
25	0.856	1.316	1.708	2.060	2.485	2.787	3.450	4.352
26	0.856	1.315	1.706	2.056	2.479	2.779	3.435	4.324
27	0.855	1.314	1.703	2.052	2.473	2.771	3.421	4.299
28	0.855	1.313	1.701	2.048	2.467	2.763	3.408	4.275
29	0.854	1.311	1.699	2.045	2.462	2.756	3.396	4.254
30	0.854	1.310	1.697	2.042	2.457	2.750	3.385	4.234
35	0.852	1.306	1.690	2.030	2.438	2.724	3.340	4.153
40	0.851	1.303	1.684	2.021	2.423	2.704	3.307	4.094
45	0.850	1.301	1.679	2.014	2.412	2.690	3.281	4.049
50	0.849	1.299	1.676	2.009	2.403	2.678	3.261	4.014
60	0.848	1.296	1.671	2.000	2.390	2.660	3.232	3.962
80	0.846	1.292	1.664	1.990	2.374	2.639	3.195	3.899
100	0.845	1.290	1.660	1.984	2.364	2.626	3.174	3.862
∞	0.842	1.282	1.645	1.960	2.327	2.576	3.091	3.720

Table of the X^2 distibution

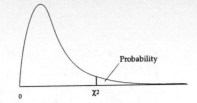

Probability (a)

df	0.995	0.99	0.9	0.1	0.05	0.025	0.01	0.005	0.001
1	0.000	0.000	0.016	2.706	3.841	5.024	6.635	7.879	10.828
2	0.010	0.020	0.211	4.605	5.991	7.378	9.210	10.597	13.816
3	0.072	0.115	0.584	6.251	7.815	9.348	11.345	12.838	16.266
4	0.207	0.297	1.064	7.779	9.488	11.143	13.277	14.860	18.467
5	0.412	0.554	1.610	9.236	11.070	12.833	15.086	16.750	20.515
6	0.676	0.872	2.204	10.645	12.592	14.449	16.812	18.548	22.458
7	0.989	1.239	2.833	12.017	14.067	16.013	18.475	20.278	24.322
8	1.344	1.646	3.490	13.362	15.507	17.535	20.090	21.955	26.124
9	1.735	2.088	4.168	14.684	16.919	19.023	21.666	23.589	27.877
10	2.156	2.558	4.865	15.987	18.307	20.483	23.209	25.188	29.588
11	2.603	3.053	5.578	17.275	19.675	21.920	24.725	26.757	31.264
12	3.074	3.571	6.304	18.549	21.026	23.337	26.217	28.300	32.909
13	3.565	4.107	7.042	19.812	22.362	24.736	27.688	29.819	34.528
14	4.075	4.660	7.790	21.064	23.685	26.119	29.141	31.319	36.123
15	4.601	5.229	8.547	22.307	24.996	27.488	30.578	32.801	37.697
16	5.142	5.812	9.312	23.542	26.296	28.845	32.000	34.267	39.252
17	5.697	6.408	10.085	24.769	27.587	30.191	33.409	35.718	40.790
18	6.265	7.015	10.865	25.989	28.869	31.526	34.805	37.156	42.312
19	6.844	7.633	11.651	27.204	30.144	32.852	36.191	38.582	43.820
20	7.434	8.260	12.443	28.412	31.410	34.170	37.566	39.997	45.315
21	8.034	8.897	13.240	29.615	32.671	35.479	38.932	41.401	46.797
22	8.643	9.542	14.041	30.813	33.924	36.781	40.289	42.796	48.268
23	9.260	10.196	14.848	32.007	35.172	38.076	41.638	44.181	49.728
24	9.886	10.856	15.659	33.196	36.415	39.364	42.980	45.559	51.179
25	0.520	11.524	16.473	34.382	37.652	40.646	44.314	46.928	52.620
26	1.160	12.198	17.292	35.563	38.885	41.923	45.642	48.290	54.052
27	1.808	12.879	18.114	36.741	40.113	43.195	46.963	49.645	55.476
28	2.461	13.565	18.939	37.916	41.337	44.461	48.278	50.993	56.892
29	3.121	14.256	19.768	39.087	42.557	45.722	49.588	52.336	58.301
30	3.787	14.953	20.599	40.256	43.773	46.979	50.892	53.672	59.703
35	7.192	18.509	24.797	46.059	49.802	53.203	57.342	60.275	66.619
40	0.707	22.164	29.051	51.805	55.758	59.342	63.691	66.766	73.402

Random Numbers

```
61 05 72 60 15 64 56 12 22 75 67 50
93 35 01 96 17 22 79 65 21 30 35 32
66 86 67 59 39 17 95 35 09 93 55 84
81 60 69 99 62 41 84 78 35 30 48 75
07 30 30 84 23 98 71 73 47 67 42 68
93 30 94 55 18 69 88 33 95 92 45 58
46 60 25 98 75 93 24 74 46 61 46 64
23 35 12 21 19 30 63 88 62 20 20 36
41 10 18 14 96 67 64 62 69 53 22 76
72 63 52 74 07 25 79 75 39 37 58 00
87 67 39 51 97 06 98 76 37 96 32 70
99 75 90 53 12 65 17 68 37 69 97 81
67 48 83 85 54 95 31 21 41 93 35 79
77 94 94 49 11 52 22 83 44 52 20 92
22 99 75 45 36 36 64 39 52 18 67 41
20 04 39 20 52 08 20 06 33 33 95 80
61 81 91 67 09 04 55 52 24 20 75 88
25 86 83 87 37 13 95 19 20 16 05 69
92 42 73 97 76 74 69 34 90 19 27 84
14 82 43 69 03 29 35 50 70 19 97 51
61 56 52 18 48 03 34 74 16 13 27 15
40 20 59 51 95 88 03 21 18 80 98 72
01 42 80 72 50 39 76 45 01 38 13 02
93 62 01 12 63 79 90 36 75 71 25 80
80 00 21 32 91 48 60 82 08 84 41 53
13 89 58 15 34 28 81 93 07 12 19 39
40 98 25 11 73 48 51 86 92 35 37 20
52 47 37 87 30 81 64 80 32 09 50 09
33 38 64 75 77 79 13 73 48 54 56 52
32 74 76 66 95 81 11 87 04 46 55 56
68 07 20 57 47 14 53 32 32 01 94 19
57 11 99 88 82 88 05 44 35 13 51 79
73 21 75 54 84 11 38 67 42 38 68 99
51 23 07 05 60 78 51 10 03 53 03 49
98 93 98 48 04 02 78 77 76 67 69 29
58 89 74 64 41 12 31 16 76 43 70 52
62 11 34 91 54 04 74 03 40 78 15 56
47 97 51 85 80 15 26 42 85 72 94 08
97 33 80 82 62 74 29 87 77 43 94 09
41 23 26 40 87 64 59 78 34 72 60 69
69 54 08 18 60 12 00 92 62 21 48 47
09 47 49 69 18 68 20 79 42 36 48 28
81 95 35 72 19 28 05 47 18 40 61 79
10 81 27 04 57 82 60 71 47 35 93 66
63 16 10 76 41 70 19 93 31 05 52 41
56 08 27 29 47 72 78 35 24 77 05 54
74 62 46 99 88 43 95 35 63 25 60 03
39 19 21 51 09 19 88 92 59 70 48 26
81 52 43 86 58 86 04 52 51 61 10 64
03 90 46 52 78 77 65 73 18 41 14 94
```

Discount factors

Discount rate	Number of years									
	1	2	3	4	5	6	7	8	9	10
0.5%	0.9950	0.9901	0.9851	0.9802	0.9754	0.9705	0.9657	0.9609	0.9561	0.9513
1.0%	0.9901	0.9803	0.9706	0.9610	0.9515	0.9420	0.9327	0.9235	0.9143	0.9053
1.5%	0.9852	0.9707	0.9563	0.9422	0.9283	0.9145	0.9010	0.8877	0.8746	0.8617
2.0%	0.9804	0.9612	0.9423	0.9238	0.9057	0.8880	0.8706	0.8535	0.8368	0.8203
2.5%	0.9756	0.9518	0.9286	0.9060	0.8839	0.8623	0.8413	0.8207	0.8007	0.7812
3.0%	0.9709	0.9426	0.9151	0.8885	0.8626	0.8375	0.8131	0.7894	0.7664	0.7441
3.5%	0.9662	0.9335	0.9019	0.8714	0.8420	0.8135	0.7860	0.7594	0.7337	0.7089
4.0%	0.9615	0.9246	0.8890	0.8548	0.8219	0.7903	0.7599	0.7307	0.7026	0.6756
4.5%	0.9569	0.9157	0.8763	0.8386	0.8025	0.7679	0.7348	0.7032	0.6729	0.6439
5.0%	0.9524	0.9070	0.8638	0.8227	0.7835	0.7462	0.7107	0.6768	0.6446	0.6139
5.5%	0.9479	0.8985	0.8516	0.8072	0.7651	0.7252	0.6874	0.6516	0.6176	0.5854
6.0%	0.9434	0.8900	0.8396	0.7921	0.7473	0.7050	0.6651	0.6274	0.5919	0.5584
6.5%	0.9390	0.8817	0.8278	0.7773	0.7299	0.6853	0.6435	0.6042	0.5674	0.5327
7.0%	0.9346	0.8734	0.8163	0.7629	0.7130	0.6663	0.6227	0.5820	0.5439	0.5083
7.5%	0.9302	0.8653	0.8050	0.7488	0.6966	0.6480	0.6028	0.5607	0.5216	0.4852
8.0%	0.9259	0.8573	0.7938	0.7350	0.6806	0.6302	0.5835	0.5403	0.5002	0.4632
8.5%	0.9217	0.8495	0.7829	0.7216	0.6650	0.6129	0.5649	0.5207	0.4799	0.4423
9.0%	0.9174	0.8417	0.7722	0.7084	0.6499	0.5963	0.5470	0.5019	0.4604	0.4224
9.5%	0.9132	0.8340	0.7617	0.6956	0.6352	0.5801	0.5298	0.4838	0.4418	0.4035
10.0%	0.9091	0.8264	0.7513	0.6830	0.6209	0.5645	0.5132	0.4665	0.4241	0.3855
10.5%	0.9050	0.8190	0.7412	0.6707	0.6070	0.5493	0.4971	0.4499	0.4071	0.3684
11.0%	0.9009	0.8116	0.7312	0.6587	0.5935	0.5346	0.4817	0.4339	0.3909	0.3522
11.5%	0.8969	0.8044	0.7214	0.6470	0.5803	0.5204	0.4667	0.4186	0.3754	0.3367
12.0%	0.8929	0.7972	0.7118	0.6355	0.5674	0.5066	0.4523	0.4039	0.3606	0.3220
12.5%	0.8889	0.7901	0.7023	0.6243	0.5549	0.4933	0.4385	0.3897	0.3464	0.3079
13.0%	0.8850	0.7831	0.6931	0.6133	0.5428	0.4803	0.4251	0.3762	0.3329	0.2946
13.5%	0.8811	0.7763	0.6839	0.6026	0.5309	0.4678	0.4121	0.3631	0.3199	0.2819
14.0%	0.8772	0.7695	0.6750	0.5921	0.5194	0.4556	0.3996	0.3506	0.3075	0.2697
14.5%	0.8734	0.7628	0.6662	0.5818	0.5081	0.4438	0.3876	0.3385	0.2956	0.2582
15.0%	0.8696	0.7561	0.6575	0.5718	0.4972	0.4323	0.3759	0.3269	0.2843	0.2472
15.5%	0.8658	0.7496	0.6490	0.5619	0.4865	0.4212	0.3647	0.3158	0.2734	0.2367
16.0%	0.8621	0.7432	0.6407	0.5523	0.4761	0.4104	0.3538	0.3050	0.2630	0.2267
16.5%	0.8584	0.7368	0.6324	0.5429	0.4660	0.4000	0.3433	0.2947	0.2530	0.2171
17.0%	0.8547	0.7305	0.6244	0.5337	0.4561	0.3898	0.3332	0.2848	0.2434	0.2080
17.5%	0.8511	0.7243	0.6164	0.5246	0.4465	0.3800	0.3234	0.2752	0.2342	0.1994
18.0%	0.8475	0.7182	0.6086	0.5158	0.4371	0.3704	0.3139	0.2660	0.2255	0.1911
18.5%	0.8439	0.7121	0.6010	0.5071	0.4280	0.3612	0.3048	0.2572	0.2170	0.1832
19.0%	0.8403	0.7062	0.5934	0.4987	0.4190	0.3521	0.2959	0.2487	0.2090	0.1756
19.5%	0.8368	0.7003	0.5860	0.4904	0.4104	0.3434	0.2874	0.2405	0.2012	0.1684
20.0%	0.8333	0.6944	0.5787	0.4823	0.4019	0.3349	0.2791	0.2326	0.1938	0.1615

Appendix 3 Mathematical and statistical formulae used in this book

Chapter 3 Summarising Data

Mean

$$\bar{x} = \frac{\sum x}{n}$$

Mean for a frequency distribution:

$$\bar{x} = \frac{\sum fx}{\sum f}$$

Standard deviation

$$\sigma = \sqrt{\frac{\sum (x - \bar{x})^2}{n}}$$

Standard deviation for a frequency distribution

$$\sigma = \sqrt{\frac{\sum fx^2}{\sum f} - \left(\frac{\sum fx}{\sum f}\right)^2}$$

Coefficient of variation

$$\frac{\text{Standard deviation}}{\text{Mean}} \times 100$$

Chapter 4 Probability and Decision-Making

Addition law

$$P(A \text{ or } B) = P(A) + P(B) - P(A \text{ and } B)$$

$$= P(A) + P(B) \text{ for mutually exclusive events}$$

Multiplication rule

$$P(A \text{ and } B) = P(A) \times P(B \mid A)$$

$$= P(A) \times P(B) \text{ for independent events}$$

Expected value

$$\sum px$$

^nC_r

$$\frac{n!}{r!(n-r)!}$$

^nP_r

$$\frac{n!}{(n-r)!}$$

Chapter 5 The normal distribution

$$z = \frac{x - \mu}{\sigma}$$

Chapter 6 Analysis and Interpretation of sample data

Point estimates for the mean and percentage

$$\mu = \bar{x} \quad \text{and} \quad \pi = p$$

Best estimate for the standard deviation

$$\sigma = s\sqrt{\frac{n}{n-1}} \quad \text{(Bessel's correction factor)}$$

Standard error of the mean

$$\text{STEM} = \frac{\sigma}{\sqrt{n}}$$

$$= \frac{2.75}{\sqrt{35}} = \frac{}{5.9161}$$

$$0.46$$

Standard error of a percentage

$$\text{STEP} = \sqrt{\frac{p(100-p)}{n}}$$

Confidence interval for a mean based on the normal distribution

$$\mu = \bar{x} \pm z \times \text{STEM}$$

Confidence interval for a mean based on the t-distribution:

$$\mu = \bar{x} \pm t \times \text{STEM}$$

Confidence interval for a percentage:

$$\pi = p \pm z \times \text{STEP}$$

Finite population correction factor:

$$\sqrt{\frac{N-n}{N-1}}$$

Chapter 7 Testing a Hypothesis

The Z-test for a sample mean

$$z = \frac{\bar{x} - \mu}{\text{STEM}}$$

The t-test for a sample mean

$$t = \frac{\bar{x} - \mu}{\text{STEM}}$$

Hypothesis test of a percentage

$$z = \frac{p - \pi}{\text{STEP}}$$

where:

$$\text{STEP} = \sqrt{\frac{\pi(100-\pi)}{n}}$$

The χ^2 hypothesis test statistic is

$$\sum \frac{(O-E)^2}{E}$$

The degrees of freedom for a goodness-of-fit test

$$n - 1 - k$$

The expected value for a contingency table is given by:

$$\text{Expected value} = \frac{\text{Row total} \times \text{Column total}}{\text{Grand total}}$$

The degrees of freedom for a contingency table is found from:

$$(\text{number of columns} - 1) \times (\text{number of rows} - 1)$$

Chapter 8 Correlation and Regression

Spearman's rank correlation coefficient

$$R = 1 - \frac{6 \sum d^2}{n(n^2 - 1)}$$

Pearson's product moment correlation coefficient

$$r = \frac{n \sum xy - \sum x \sum y}{\sqrt{\left(n \sum x^2 - \left(\sum x\right)^2\right)\left(n \sum y^2 - \left(\sum y\right)^2\right)}}$$

Line of best fit (method of least squares)

$$Y = a + b\,X$$

The values of 'a' and 'b' that minimise the squared errors are given by the equations:

$$b = \frac{n \sum xy - \sum x \sum y}{n \sum x^2 - \left(\sum x\right)^2}$$

$$a = \frac{\sum y}{n} - b \frac{\sum x}{n}$$

The coefficient of determination

$$r^2$$

Index